FALCONS
of North America

KATE DAVIS

Photographs by Rob Palmer and Nick Dunlop

2008
Mountain Press Publishing Company
Missoula, Montana

Photographs © 2008 by Rob Palmer and Nick Dunlop except as noted

Front cover photo: American Kestrel by Rob Palmer
Back cover photos:
Top: Aplomado Falcon by Rob Palmer
Middle: Gyrfalcon by Rob Palmer
Bottom: Peregrine Falcon by Nick Dunlop

Library of Congress Cataloging-in-Publication Data

Davis, Kate, 1959–
  Falcons of North America / by Kate Davis ; photographs by Rob Palmer
and Nick Dunlop
      p. cm.
  Includes bibliographical references and index.
  ISBN 978-0-87842-553-2 (pbk. : alk. paper)
  1. Falcons—North America. I. Title.
  QL696.F34D38 2009
  598.9'6097—dc22

                        2008032342

PRINTED IN CANADA BY FRIESENS

Mountain Press Publishing Company
P.O. Box 2399
Missoula, Montana 59806

To the memory of my father,
Carlos Phillips, my *first* hero.

A Peregrine Falcon in the Bitterroot. —KATE DAVIS

Adult female Peregrine Falcon. —NICK DUNLOP

Contents

A trained Peregrine lands. —KATE DAVIS

Preface

My introduction to the world of raptors came from reading a book called *My Side of the Mountain*. I immediately wanted to run away from home, live in a hollow tree, and fly a trained Peregrine Falcon. Many years after reading Jean Craighead George's book, I was in the audience at a lecture by her brother John J. Craighead and was enthralled by his stories of the wild grizzly bears of Montana. I grew up in the suburbs of Cincinnati, and inspired by these adventurous tales, I decided that I would move to Montana and study birds. Little did I know that some thirty years later I would be privileged to spend a day in the field with a falcon and the Craighead family.

My experience suggests the power one book can have over a young and malleable mind. I knew early on that somehow I was going to surround myself with animals. In 1973 at age thirteen I was fortunate enough to join the Junior Zoologists Club at the Cincinnati Zoo. Again, one person was to shape me forever: Education Director Barry Wakeman. I was immediately immersed in a life of wildlife rehabilitation, education, taxidermy, wildlife art, and falconry.

I moved to Montana in 1978 and earned a degree in zoology from the University of Montana in 1982. In 1988 I began an educational program that came to be called Raptors of the Rockies, and surround myself with animals I did—raptors, to be exact. I have been privileged to be able to keep rehabilitated hawks, eagles, and owls that are ambassadors in educational programs around the state. But my favorites have always been the falcons, ever since flying a kestrel as a teenager in Ohio. Since that early age I have been reading about, speaking about, photographing, depicting in art, and now writing a book about falcons. And for the majority of that time writing, I have had jazz on the stereo, reference materials piled high, and a Peregrine Falcon named Sibley perched here in the living room with me.

In 2004 I had just begun volunteering for the Montana Peregrine Institute but had been friends with the director, Jay Sumner, for almost twenty years. I was enlisted to observe Peregrine nest sites to record occupancy (if both adults were present) and productivity (counting young on the ledge or fledglings). When I was flying my bird Sibley at a nearby property, a juvenile Peregrine sometimes joined us, begging and harassing my bird, and I reported it to Jay.

Bright and early one morning in April 2005 we hiked up that drainage in the Bitterroot Mountains of Western Montana with hopes of locating a new Peregrine nest, or eyrie. On the walk up, motion caught my eye and we saw a Peregrine pair chasing a songbird right through the tree canopy. Minutes later we spotted both adult falcons perched on a snag at the top of a cliff, silhouetted against the skyline. We watched them escort an adult Golden Eagle from the area with a hearty tap, an eagle feather flying. What a cause for celebration—we had found the new breeding territory. There were no breeding records for Peregrines in the Bitterroot Valley before the DDT era (although they might have bred and were not documented) and the species was gone from the state from the 1960s until the early 1980s and a big reintroduction effort. Our discovery was big news: it made the eleventh known nest in the Bitterroot, making the valley an official hotbed of breeding activity. The "icing on the gravy" was that when I turned the spotting scope 180 degrees from the cliff face, I could see my driveway and house across the valley!

In the hundreds of hours gazing at cliffs, Jay and I talked about our influences, and I found that John and Frank Craighead were his mentors and dear friends. I told him that John had sparked my interest in Montana in the first place. We thought, let's get John to come out in the field to fly our Peregrines at the place where we had found the new eyrie. Great idea—and wonder of wonders, it really happened.

The beautiful fall day came, and we hosted John and his wife, Margaret, and son, Johnny. We loaded Jay's young Peregrine and my three-year-old bird, Sibley, in the Subaru and headed to the exercise grounds across the road. Jay flew his bird first and she made some great passes at the lure; then it was Sibley's turn. She had been a little territorial in the past at her training hill, swiping hats off the heads of bystanders on occasion. While I was hailed as a great trainer for having her perform such a novel trick, for me that stunt was just bad, bad, bad. I was trembling as I attached the transmitters and told her to be good, get high, and for God's sake, don't try to hit John Craighead. I prayed she would behave herself as we cut her loose with the Craighead family nearby.

Up she went, and after a few circles I heard John say that it was like the old days. As an almost surreal boost to our enjoyment of watching Sib, a wild adult Peregrine came from nowhere to join her in some high laps of almost synchronized flight. The two falcons spent several minutes overhead before I called Sibley down, and the wild bird headed off across the valley. It was a peaceful moment before the appearance of game. Sibley hit a pheasant in a nice stoop and knocked it to our feet. I was so relieved that the only blood of the day would be avian, and what a huge honor to have our guru, mentor, and hero present. With his smile and faraway look, I imagined John was reliving a much more spectacular falcon hunt from the skies—a vertical stoop from a thousand feet, an image that was etched in his memory forever.

For anyone who has seen a falcon in its element of the air, it is an emotional experience that will never cease to amaze. Falcons' mastery of the skies and spectacle in flight has rightfully earned them a place as natural icons. For many of us, falcons are the Pinnacle of Perfection.

A falcon flies over the Bitterroot Mountains of Montana. —KATE DAVIS

Acknowledgments

This account of North American falcons would not have been possible without the help of Joel "jeep" Pagel and his thorough edits of the main chapters. His vast knowledge, experience, and insight are very much appreciated. Thanks also to Dan Varland, who had an early look at the entire manuscript and provided brilliant help and guidance. Many thanks to Donna Lucey, my literary guru and advisor from afar.

Many others in the field were enlisted for their expertise, and I thank R. Wayne Nelson, Ian Newton, Karen Steenhof, Travis Booms, Jemima Parry-Jones, Glenn Stewart, Steve Hoffman, Dick Hutto, Gary Santolo, Dale Becker, Brian Latta, Janet Linthicum, Jessi Brown, Bruce Haak, Chuck Henny and Rick Harness. Bud Anderson of the Falcon Research Group took time out of his hectic field season tracking Peregrines to help us greatly with the Falcon Movements chapter (not to mention giving me some appreciated words of encouragement).

We are pleased and honored to be able to use the fine paper on nest observation protocols by Richard Fyfe and the late Richard "Butch" Olendorff.

Our photographers are the finest. Thanks to my good friend Rob Palmer for his exemplary work (and advice). Nick Dunlop's fantastic signature shots of wild falcons grace these pages, and with these two photographers, we have a one-of-a-kind book!

Our other photographers are some of the best in the field. We are lucky to have shots by Will Sooter, Bob Steele, Ron Austing, Jon Avery, Kenny Sterner, Glenn Stewart, Evet Loewen, Glenn Nevill, Tracy Fleming, Jeep Pagel, Scott Francis, and Bob Tabke.

Thanks to Brian Wheeler for allowing me to use his range maps from his two *Raptors of North America* books as guides for ours. And we appreciate Mark Proster's Southern Cross Peregrine Project map of Sparky's travels. And thanks to Gale Johnson, my computer guru, for construction tips.

For inspiration, I have to thank Tom Cade for his book *The Falcons of the World* and Hans Peeters for the real page-turner *Raptors of California*.

I appreciate the help, guidance, and generosity of these Friends of Falcons! Any errors that appear on these pages are purely my own.

The Prairie Falcon is the true North American resident, indigenous to the western part of the continent, and the logo for the Raptor Research Foundation for the last four decades.
—ROB PALMER

Introduction

There is nothing like it. Nothing on earth. A distant falcon suddenly makes a decision and takes action, dropping thousands of feet from the sky to pursue an unknowing—then panicking—bird fleeing for its life. The sound of the falcon *whooshing*, feet thrown forward, the violent contact and sudden explosion of feathers; then the falcon rolls over in flight to move in for the final grab. After landing the falcon pants, catches her breath, shakes her feathers, repositions her feet, and settles in for a meal. You've witnessed one of the most venerable feats in the natural world.

Falcons may be the super-raptor, or topmost of the predatory birds. They live everywhere in the world except Antarctica, in every habitat from desert to tropical forest. Several species thrive in cities, nesting on human-made structures and feeding on pigeons and starlings. Falcons are a highly successful family of birds that have been admired by people for millennia.

Raptors are birds of prey—predators that rely on finding, catching, and killing other animals for food. In North America, raptors range in size from the diminutive Elf Owl gleaning insects off leaves to the huge Golden Eagle in high-speed pursuit of a racing jackrabbit. Two orders, or groups, of birds make up the raptors. The order Strigiformes encompasses the owls, which are mainly nocturnal (active at night), and the order Falconiformes, which means "falcon shaped," is made up of the diurnal (daytime) raptors: falcons and caracaras (family Falconidae); hawks, eagles, harriers, kites, buzzards, and Old World vultures (family Accipitridae); the Osprey (family Pandionidae); New World vultures and condors (family Cathartidae); and the Secretary Bird (family Sagittariidae). Strigiformes and Falconiformes are probably not closely related, although some researchers believe that because of structural and behavioral traits, falcons may be more closely related to owls than to the hawks and eagles. Strigiformes and Falconiformes have similar adaptations because of convergent evolution. This means that with the shared need to kill prey, these two unrelated groups (orders) have developed comparable physical adaptations, anatomical structures, and behaviors to help them accomplish the job of hunting and killing prey.

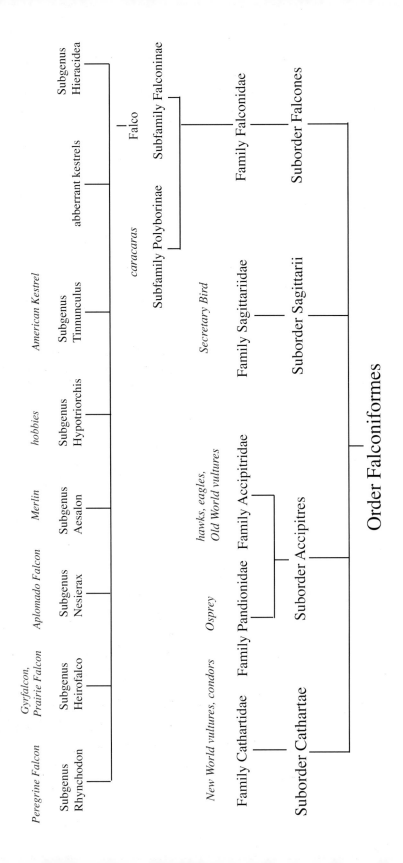

Within the order Falconiformes, the family Accipitridae (hawks) is thought to have evolved before the family Falconidae. The fossil record indicates that the first birds of prey evolved in early Eocene time (55 to 34 million years ago). Falcons evolved about 20 million years ago, which is recent in the evolution of vertebrates. All members of the genus *Falco* are closely related, originating in late Pliocene and Pleistocene time, with no fossils of contemporary species existing before 2 million years ago. Although biologists can only speculate where falcons originated geographically, the fossil record shows that falcons spread rapidly throughout the world. This may be because vast areas of forest were opened to grassland and savannah after a drastic change in the climate.

The family Falconidae encompasses about sixty species: all of the falcons, forest-falcons, falconets, and caracaras. This last taxon is very different from the true falcons. Caracaras are rather slow fliers and opportunists; and many species are omnivores, eating just about anything edible, including coconuts. They often forage on foot on the ground, feeding on carrion and roadkill. They also build their own nests, using small sticks placed in cactuses or small trees. Nine caracara species live in Central and South America, with only the Crested Caracara inhabiting North America and making it into Florida and Texas in the United States.

A Gyrfalcon eyrie is located on an isolated outcrop near Nome, Alaska. —ROB PALMER

Technological advances in DNA studies have recently stirred the world of research in avian evolution. A study published in June of 2008 challenges the long-believed position of falcons in the tree of life. By analyzing the hereditary information encoded in the DNA (genomes) of birds from over sixty living groups, relationships have been reevaluated. Instead of being classified with the hawks, falcons (the family Falconidae) were found to be in a separate group, more closely related to parrots, and nearly as highly evolved as passerines (perching birds such as songbirds). This new grouping suggests that the raptorial lifestyle evolved several times. Research will continue, and current classification work will probably result in a whole new family tree for birds.

Crested Caracaras are in the falcon family but are very different from birds in the genus Falco. *They often run on the ground and scavenge both plant and animal matter.* —ROB PALMER

Biologists use a system of scientific names (binomial nomenclature) to classify all living things. These names are also called Latin names because they are often derived from Latin or Greek. They are recognized worldwide, and consist of a genus name followed by a species name; a subspecies will also have a subspecies name. The genus name for true falcons, *Falco*, is from the Latin for "sickle." The origin of the name is not clear, but it is believed to refer to the wing shape, or perhaps the curved beak or talons. The species name designates a group within the genus whose members are closely related. For example, *Falco femoralis* is the Latin name for the Aplomado Falcon. In North America there are six species in the genus *Falco*: American Kestrel, Merlin, Aplomado Falcon, Prairie Falcon, Peregrine Falcon, and Gyrfalcon.

Cliff updrafts ruffle the feathers of a Prairie Falcon as it surveys the valley below. —NICK DUNLOP

 # TAXONOMY

Kingdom	*Animalia*
Phylum	*Chordata*, animals with a notochord associated with a backbone
Class	*Aves*, the birds
Order	*Falconiformes*, the falcons, hawks, eagles, Ospreys, Old World vultures, and Secretary Birds
Family	*Falconidae*, the falcons
Genus	*Falco*
Species	*columbarius*
Subspecies	*suckleyi*
Common name	Black or Pacific Merlin

A Black Merlin with a captured blackbird. Merlins were formerly called Pigeon Hawks because their flight style is similar to birds in the pigeon and dove family.
—NICK DUNLOP

Until the 1950s many North American falcons had common names that were misleading, often including the word *hawk*, and some common names referred to completely different birds. A Pigeon Hawk could be a Sharp-shinned Hawk or a Merlin, and the Duck Hawk was a bird famous for hunting ducks—the Peregrine. Sparrowhawk was used to refer to the American Kestrel but more accurately refers to a group of nineteen species of Old World accipiter hawks, including the widespread Eurasian Sparrowhawk. Ornithologists officially changed the common names of these birds to avoid confusion and to be universal.

The common and scientific names used today are often descriptive of the species' ranges, behaviors, or appearances. For example, American Kestrel and Prairie Falcon have names that reflect where they live, and Aplomado comes from Spanish, referring to the color of lead, a dark slate gray that dominates the Aplomado Falcon's plumage. Peregrine means "wanderer," and the Merlin's species name, *columbarius*, means "like a pigeon." Gyrfalcon may come from Latin meaning "sacred falcon." Indeed these birds are all revered by many, from occasional birdwatchers to researchers, scientists, and falconers around the world. Their attraction is cosmopolitan and contagious for anyone who has seen them in action: the super-raptor of the natural world.

A Peregrine pursues some ducks. The hen Mallard nearest the falcon is flying upside down to avoid capture. —KATE DAVIS

— 1 —
Falcon Morphology and Physiology

Living things are classified into groups by genetics, morphology (physical structure and anatomy), or both. *Morph-* means "form" and *-ology* means "the study of." Descriptions of falcons are of a streamlined raptor with long, narrow, curved wings, a compact body, and swift flight capabilities. Falcons are mostly denizens of vast landscapes, open country, and big sky. But falcons can and do use wooded habitat and will venture into the forest canopy, chasing prey or perching silently before or after hunting. Falcons are mostly diurnal, or active during the day.

Smallest of the North American falcons is the colorful American Kestrel, commonly seen bobbing its head and tail while perched on telephone lines or fences. The Merlin is slightly larger and stockier and may frequent bird feeders to catch songbirds. The next larger is the Aplomado Falcon, a resident from the southern edge of the United States south to suitable areas of Mexico and Central and South America. The northern subspecies of Aplomado is considered endangered. The Prairie Falcon is endemic (native) to the dry, open spaces of western North America. About the same size is the Peregrine Falcon, a bird that once faced extinction in North America but has made a remarkable comeback. The largest of North American falcons is the Gyrfalcon, an Arctic breeder that migrates to the southern Canadian provinces and northern tier of the United States during the winter.

Falcons are powerful flyers. *Wing loading* is the term used to describe the ratio of body weight to wing surface area; falcons have high wing loading. This means they have larger body weight (mass) supported by a small surface area. Falcons are described as bullet shaped and possess large pectoral muscles attached to a uniquely structured breastbone. These flight muscles make up 12 percent of the overall body weight of a kestrel and up to 20 percent for a Peregrine. Generally, falcons have a wide-ranging hunting area and pursue their prey in aerial attacks, often chasing their quarry for long distances in high-speed flight. This would be difficult for most hawks.

Falcons lack the large, bony, overhanging brow that gives hawks and eagles a fierce appearance. With just a slight brow, the entire falcon eye is visible. Most falcon species have a malar stripe, a darker area just below the eye.

FALCON TOPOGRAPHY

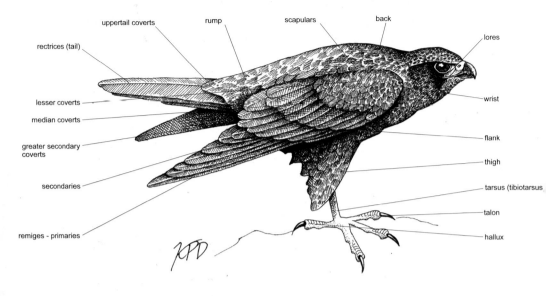

uppertail coverts — rump — scapulars — back — lores

rectrices (tail)

lesser coverts

median coverts

greater secondary coverts

secondaries

remiges - primaries

wrist

flank

thigh

tarsus (tibiotarsus

talon

hallux

A female American Kestrel perches on a fence. American Kestrels are often seen scanning the ground from a telephone or power line, and they may pursue prey flushed by a moving vehicle. —ROB PALMER

Some references call it a "mustache," especially for the Prairie Falcon. One theory is that this stripe conceals the eye and contributes to the bird's disruptive coloration, or camouflage, making it unclear which direction the bird is looking. This form of concealment is widespread in many predatory birds, and also predatory mammals such as large cats. The dark patch might also reduce glare, a property exploited by some football players who put black greasepaint under their eyes.

Falcons worldwide (with the exception of some forest-falcons and a single kestrel in Africa) have dark brown irises and black pupils, giving them a very dark eye. Falcons have bare skin around their eyes called the orbital ring, which in many species changes color with age and diet. The orbital ring can change from a pale blue to yellow and sometimes even orange in the males after a year of age. To some species, bright colors are attractive in courtship and breeding. The cere is the bare area at the base of the upper mandible, where the nostrils are located. Made of keratin, it shares the same protein structure as feathers and skin. The cere also changes color with age, or sometimes simply deepens in color intensity. These facial field marks often contrast with the plumage. The skin color of the legs also changes with age and diet, from pale blue the first year to yellow and orange the second year in most species, or third year for Gyrfalcons.

A young Richardson's Merlin. The tomial tooth located just behind the sharp point of the beak is used to break the neck of prey. —NICK DUNLOP

The eyes of a Prairie Falcon are the largest in proportion to the head of any falcon. The proportion is greatest for the male (shown here), whose eyes are about the same size as the larger female.
—KATE DAVIS

Falcon nostrils, or nares, are unique structures that morphologically distinguish them from all other raptors. The nostril opening is round rather than elongate, as in most other raptors, and has a central bony knob called a tubercle, or cone. This central structure has also been called a baffle and may break up the air current flowing over the beak during fast flight, making it easier for the falcon to breathe during high-speed dives. Another suggestion is that these baffles might sense changes in air speed, pressure, or temperature. New research shows that this tubercle helps to regulate the direct flow of air into the lungs and air sacs.

WEAPONS

A bird's beak, or bill, is made up of the upper mandible, or maxilla, and the lower mandible, both covered in horny sheaths. The structure and size of the beak are adaptations to feeding habits. All raptors have a curved, hooked beak with sharp cutting edges designed for a meat diet. Falcons have short necks with fifteen cervical vertebrae (long-necked birds have twenty-five). They also have short beaks, complete with muscles to deliver a powerful bite.

PRAIRIE FALCON HEAD

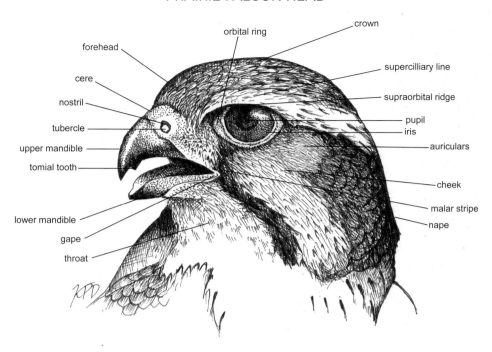

The falcon beak has a unique structure called a tomial tooth on the maxilla that corresponds to a notch in the lower mandible. These two surfaces create a cutting mechanism to sever the spinal cord of the prey. Either the prey is killed right away or the central nervous system is badly damaged, preventing escape. Captive falcons frequently bite the neck of dead quail before feeding. Falcons can decapitate a bird in seconds, even in flight—sometimes the head of the prey is seen falling from the sky. Some falcons may pluck and eat a small bird without ever landing.

Raptors have a specialized tendon configuration in their feet to permit a powerful grip on their prey after it has been seized. Strong muscles in the upper leg pull the toes in with long flexor tendons. These track through tough sheaths of skin and muscle with ridges on the underside of the foot. The corresponding ridges on the tendons create what Nick Fox called a "ratchet mechanism," which locks like a hand brake on a car, allowing the raptor to maintain a tight grip on its prey with minimal energy expenditure.

A hawk or eagle will spasmodically squeeze prey to death with its power-ful feet. But a falcon's feet are built to hold prey while it uses the tomial tooth to deliver a fatal bite to the neck.

RETICULATE FALCON FOOT

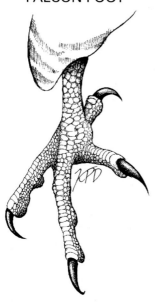

Falcons have reticulate feet—the small scales on the surface are irregular and net-like, or reticulated. Prey birds have loose, shifting feathers, and many times prey will lose a big patch of feathers, or even all of the tail, rather than get caught. A chase may result in nothing more than a foot full of feathers for the falcon. The undersides of a falcon's toes have bulbous knobs, or digital pads, that help maintain a secure grip on the feathers of the prey. Accipiters, such as the Sharp-shinned Hawk, and other raptors that hunt birds also have these knobs on their feet. The middle toe of a falcon is especially long, hinting at how important it is for grasping. A study of ninety Peregrines found the scale pattern on this toe allows for identification of individuals, a unique "fingerprint"—or, in this case, footprint.

EYES AND VISION

Raptors have at least two and a half—perhaps even as much as six to eight—times the visual acuity (ability to distinguish details) of humans; theirs is possibly the most acute vision in the animal world. Plus they have "fast" vision, or the ability to assimilate detail rapidly, which is essential for flight. Frank Gill stated that birds are able to "capture at a glance a whole picture rather than to piece a scene together after a laborious scan, as humans do." In addition to excellent long-distance vision, falcons see well up close. After feeding, they meticulously pick tiny food morsels from their feet and surroundings.

Falcons have huge eyeballs to collect available light. Their eyes are fifteen times proportionally larger than those of humans. Like all bird eyes, falcon eyes are not spherical but rather flattened and strengthened with a ring of twelve to fifteen small bony plates called the scleral ossicles, or sclerotic ring. The dinosaur ancestors of birds also had sclerotic rings. Raptor eyes are fixed in the skull and have limited movement in the eye socket, unlike the eyes of mammals. Two sets of muscles (Crampton's and Brucke's) attach to these rings: the Crampton's controls the curvature of the cornea and the Brucke's controls the lens. In this way the eye focuses on an object or scene. The Crampton's muscles are especially developed in raptors.

The retina is on the rear surface of the eye. It collects light that has passed through the cornea, lens, and pupil to form an image; the optic nerve

Peregrine Falcons, like all raptors, have forward-facing eyes and binocular vision.
—KATE DAVIS

The nares with baffles and eye ring of a young Gyrfalcon. —KATE DAVIS

then transmits this information to the brain. Two types of photoreceptive cells—cones and rods—lie on the retina. Cones specialize in daylight (color) vision, and rods are simple light receptors specializing in black-and-white, and therefore night vision. Cones are more numerous in the eyes of diurnal birds (up to 80 percent of the cells), while rods are more numerous in nocturnal birds, such as owls and the goatsucker family (Whip-poor-wills and Nighthawks). The human eye has two hundred thousand cones per square millimeter, whereas a large hawk (any member of the genus *Buteo*) has over a million of these cells per square millimeter. It is comparable to the number of pixels on a computer screen, or a newsprint photo versus a glossy print: raptors are on the high-resolution end.

All raptors have forward-facing eyes with an overlap between their left and right fields of vision. Using both eyes together, they have binocular overlap vision of 35 to 50 degrees. In their field of view with this overlap, they are able to see depth of field and distance. Prey birds have eyes laterally located on the sides of their heads in order to detect danger from any direction. They can see up to 360 degrees, but only with monocular vision.

Like hawks and owls, falcons bob their heads, moving them back and forth, and up and down. This is a common behavior of the American Kestrel. While it may appear that a bird is acting out of curiosity when it bobs its

A young Richardson's Merlin lands near the nest. This subspecies usually has four light tail bars, five including the tip. —ROB PALMER

The nictitating membrane flashes across the eye of a Prairie Falcon. —KATE DAVIS

head, this motion actually allows a raptor to see an object from many different angles and judge its distance. The head bobbing utilizes motion parallax, the phenomenon in which an object seems to move against a stationary background as the viewer's position changes. By moving the location of the eyes (which are fixed in the eye sockets) the raptor can improve its judgment of the distance of prey—or potential predators. Objects that are closer move more quickly across the field of view than those farther away, like distant trees and hills.

Birds have a third eyelid called the nictitating membrane, or membrana nictitans. This type of membrane is also found in fish, reptiles, and amphibians. In most mammals it is vestigial and without apparent function, located on the inside corners of the eyes. The nictitating membrane is opaque in owls and somewhat transparent in most other birds. When birds blink, the thin membrane flashes quickly across the eye surface laterally. The membrane moisturizes, cleans, and protects the eye. It originates at the inside corner and has T-shaped cartilage to support the leading edge. Blinking is controlled by a very long tendon that wraps around the entire eye.

The nictitating membrane brushes secretions across the cornea, or eye surface. Falcon tears are viscous and less likely to dry out than human tears, as they must keep the eye moist in flight. The lacrimal, or tear, gland is in the ventral (forward) rim of the orbit (eye socket). Like most birds, falcons have a second secretory gland, the Harderian, but it is especially developed in falcons. The Harderian gland is thought to produce the substance that lessens tear evaporation, important during high-speed falcon flight.

The inside surface of the nictitating membrane is covered with unique structures called feather epithelia, which are especially robust in Peregrines. These brushlike projections serve to clean the eye surface. Any foreign matter is swept away and tears are spread across the eye. The nictitating membrane also offers protection from debris in the air, especially during flight. For raptors an important function is that it also guards against eye damage that might occur on impact with live prey.

Birds have a unique structure inside their eye called the pecten. It is composed of blood vessels and connective tissues, and often described as comparable to a pleated accordion or a steam radiator. This structure is largest in diurnal raptors and is found in the posterior chamber of the eye on the retina, standing upright and attached to the optic nerve. The pecten consists of rather large capillaries (blood vessels) matted together. Theories on its function vary but include improving sensitivity to small moving objects. The pecten rises at a right angle to the retina, and light causes shadows to be cast on the gridlike retinal surface, possibly enhancing detection of movement. Another theory suggests that it aids in navigation and is the center for magnetic sensitivity. Because of its vascular quality, the pecten probably supplies nutrients and oxygen to the retina through osmosis, or passive fluid transfer though a porous membrane.

High-speed flight is aided by a specialized avian eye. Falcons and other diurnal raptors, along with terns, hummingbirds, swallows, swifts, and kingfishers, must judge speed and distance quickly. All of these birds have two distinct places—called the central and temporal foveas—in each eye where the image is formed. The foveas are found on the retinal surface on the back of the eye. Lined with very dense concentrations of the daylight visual receptor cones, each fovea lies in a concave depression. One theory is that two foveas may cause birds to see two images of the same object at the same time, with the brain interpreting the view as a stereoscopic 3-D picture.

The central (or deep) fovea has the densest concentration of photoreceptors in the avian eye. It allows the bird to sense movement quickly but is monocular, with no overlap between left and right eyes. Sight with the central fovea is directed to the sides, approximately 45 degrees from the central axis of the bird's body. The second focusing point is the temporal fovea, also called the lateral or shallow fovea. It allows binocular vision and forward-directed sight.

A hawk or falcon may view distant objects with the head held sideways, using the central fovea to see a clear monocular image. It can change its head

FALCON SKULL WITH CENTRAL AND TEMPORAL FOVEAS

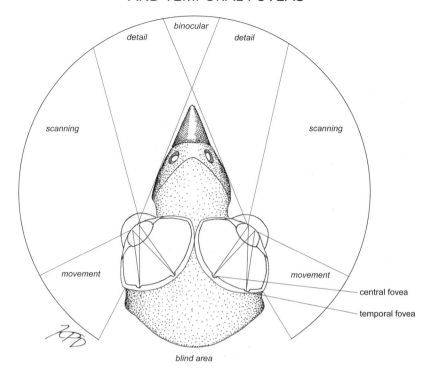

positions continuously to view alternately with the central and temporal fovea. Sometimes it will turn its head upside down to get a better look at a bird in the sky overhead. Distance is gauged using the temporal fovea and binocular vision. Diurnal raptors also have more photoreceptors in the upper half of the retina, which helps them gain a sharper image when scanning the sky.

Peregrines are able to hunt at 3,000 feet (nearly 1,000 meters) or more above their prey so as not to be observed. Recent studies with Peregrines have shown that by having the highest magnification in the central area of the eye, they can best observe distant prey by holding their heads at about a 40-degree angle, since the eyes are fixed in the sockets. Using the central fovea, falcons can spot birds from over a mile away. However, to be aerodynamic the head must be held straight forward: this position is essential for a high-speed dive and fast flight.

Tests of falcon and hawk models in wind tunnels suggest a head turn of 40 degrees results in a 50 percent increase in drag, slowing the bird's speed by half—a tremendous handicap. A Peregrine flies with head held straight, and

A shallow-angle stoop of a Peregrine Falcon. Falcons make minute changes in their body shape, stretching and streamlining, and are capable of speeds over 200 miles per hour (320 km/h).
—ROB PALMER

instead of a direct approach it takes a curved or spiral dive, sometimes called a corkscrew. In this way it keeps the prey in sight with the central fovea at all times. Interestingly, this is the mathematical ideal path, sometimes called the logarithmic spiral; it is the most efficient way of travel. Flying in a curve increases the distance to the prey, but the advantages of the aerodynamic flight with head pointing forward and less drag more than make up for the longer distance. When the falcon is close to the prey, distance is better perceived with the binocular vision of the temporal fovea. At this last approach, the flight path straightens out. A curved path also may fool the prey, which would be alarmed with a direct approach flight.

The high-speed, three-dimensional world of flight also requires a brain that can process visual information and react extremely rapidly. The human brain is able to perceive about twenty events per second, so when a film is projected at twenty-four frames per second we perceive the separate still images as smooth, continuous motion. This perception is called flicker fusion frequency (FFF), which is a measurement of the number of images per second that the brain perceives as one steady picture rather than separate, flickering

This young Peregrine is selecting a shorebird from a huge flock. Both predator and prey display lightning-fast reflexes, and more often than not, the attack is unsuccessful. —NICK DUNLOP

images. Raptors can see seventy to eighty images per second, perceiving events closer together in time. They live in a different world, perceiving events more quickly and clearly than people can, giving them the tools they need for rapid maneuvering during pursuit of prey. Perhaps human race car drivers, downhill ski racers, and jet fighter pilots also have "quicker" brains—giving new meaning to the term *birdbrain*.

Raptors' levels of adrenal hormones fluctuate so that in situations requiring rapid reactions, their FFF increases and their hearing improves. They also have well-developed organs of balance that allow them to keep their head, and thus their eyes, horizontal in nearly all situations—whether perching on a limb in the wind, chasing prey, or hovering in flight.

Some falcons have been shown to see ultraviolet light. Visible light exists in a spectrum of wavelengths. Humans cannot detect ultraviolet light, but some birds can. Like its North American counterpart the American Kestrel, the Common Kestrel of Europe hunts for rodents in open grasslands and agricultural fields. This terrain is often vast and featureless, making it difficult to locate prey. Common Kestrels have been shown to use clues left by rodents to narrow their search. Small mammals mark their trails and territories with urine, which is visible to kestrels as ultraviolet light. Kestrels cue in on these ultraviolet trails to concentrate their hunting activities at busy "intersections."

An American Kestrel eats a newly caught vole. The Common Kestrel of Europe is able to track rodents by seeing the ultraviolet markings left on their urine trails. Perhaps other falcon species share this skill.
—NICK DUNLOP

OTHER SENSES

Raptors have excellent hearing. Some owls can locate prey by sound alone. Diurnal raptors can differentiate among extremely similar sounds, some of which the human ear is unable to detect. Raptors can also distinguish between sounds that are very close in time (0.6 to 2.5 milliseconds apart). Raptors use sounds to locate the source of an animal's distress call or rustling vegetation. However, hawks and falcons are probably unable to detect sound in wavelengths lower than those detected by humans.

Like most birds, falcons have less developed senses of taste and smell than mammals do. While humans have about ten thousand taste buds, most birds have fewer than one hundred, located mostly on the rear of the tongue. They do have scent-detecting cells in the third, or last, chamber of the nostril. Falcons are probably not able to pick up scents from the air but are able to smell and taste food. When captive raptors sample a meal, they sometimes find meat distasteful and spit it out. Even when the meat is held at the tip of the beak, they will flick it away, probably able to pick up the disagreeable scent of an unpalatable food item. Since they do not need it for finding prey, the sense of smell is not as important and therefore not as highly developed in falcons as in some other birds.

The avian sense of touch is difficult for humans to gauge, but it is certainly important to falcons. Like other birds, they are able to feel changes in the air and wind around them. A specialized feather called a filoplume is involved in this process. Filoplumes are long and hairlike with small bristles at their tips. They always lie near other feathers and probably sense movement of the host feather. Nerve endings at the base of each filoplume register these changes, allowing the falcon to react to wind currents.

FLIGHT

Flying is an extremely strenuous activity. Although other groups of animals have attained powered flight (insects, bats, extinct pterosaurs), birds have evolved complex adaptations well suited to the demands of life in the air. Even among other birds, falcons are considered superb aerialists.

Flight is a balance between keeping the bird's weight in the air and maintaining forward momentum by overcoming the forces of gravity and drag, or air resistance. Birds combine high power with low body weight to maintain flight. Flight muscles are large and centrally located, but the hollow, porous bones and internal organs are lightweight. Drag is reduced through the streamlining of overall body shape. The process of wing flapping doesn't push the bird up in the air by driving the air downward, as one might think. Instead, air currents flowing over and under the wing surface cause lift through a process called the Bernoulli effect. The teardrop profile of the top of the wing causes air flowing over it to speed up, resulting in a drop in pressure. The concave undersurface causes air to slow down, which increases pressure. Combining these two forces results in lift, making flight possible.

Two measurements are used to describe wings: wing loading and aspect ratio. Wing loading describes a bird's weight versus the surface area of its outstretched wings. Falcons have small wings relative to their body mass and thus high wing loading. In contrast, vultures have large wings relative to body mass and therefore low wing loading. Aspect ratio describes wing length versus width; falcons, with relatively long, narrow wings, have a high aspect ratio, while vultures have a low aspect ratio. In cross section, falcon wings have a flattish profile, called low camber. The result is the classic falcon shape for high-speed flight. Other birds that share this flight style and wing shape are the swallows, swifts, shorebirds, pigeons and doves, and hummingbirds. In his 1967 book *The Peregrine*, John Alec Baker described falcons as a "cloud-biting anchor shape." Falcon flight is impressive, be it the hovering of an American Kestrel, the fast, coursing flight of a Prairie Falcon, or the dashing chase of a Merlin.

Feathers are unique to birds and may have evolved from reptilian scales. Like most other avian physical features, feathers are lightweight. Falcon feathers are

VENTRAL VIEW OF WINGS

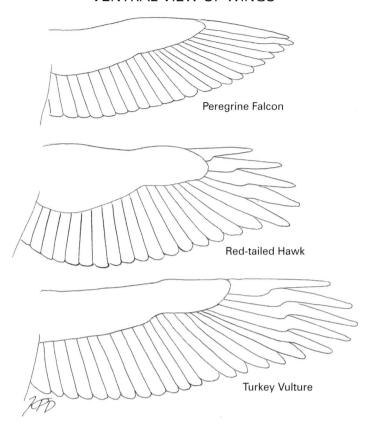

Peregrine Falcon

Red-tailed Hawk

Turkey Vulture

stiff, creating a sleek and compact surface. In contrast, the feathers on an accipiter are soft so that they don't break as the bird crashes through the forest and brush. Falcons tend to hunt in open country, with fewer opportunities for feather damage. These stiff falcon flight feathers actually vibrate and in a fast dive make a sound described as "tearing a sheet of canvas." Few people (or birds) who have heard this sound will ever forget it, although for the prey it is usually too late.

Flight feathers (remiges) are attached to bones on the wing at roughly right angles when the wing is opened in flight. Falcons have ten primary flight feathers attached to the bones of the hand, or manus. Only the last two feathers at the wingtip are slotted, or emarginated, on the outer part of the web of skin between the bones, a characteristic associated with high-speed flight. Soaring raptors with low wing loading, such as eagles, vultures, and buteos,

An Aplomado Falcon in flight, displaying the primary and secondary feathers of the wing (remiges) and tail feathers (rectrices). —ROB PALMER

have a greater number of slotted primaries, which are "notched" on the inner web. These modified primary feathers act as individual winglets to counteract stalling, allowing for low-speed soaring flight. Falcons can soar by changing their wing shape. The twelve secondary feathers of falcons are attached to the forearm bone, also called the ulna.

Birds also have a "bastard wing," or alula (alulae in plural), which serves dual purposes for falcons. These small quill feathers attach to the first digit, or thumb, and rest on the topside of the wing. When the wing angle increases, as in a slow glide, turbulent air passes over the top surface of the wing. The bird then flares the alulae, creating a slot that steadily "smoothes" the air, thus avoiding a stall. Falcons also make minute adjustments to the alulae in high-speed dives, or stoops, to increase mobility.

Food is transferred between Peregrines during courtship. Note the flared alula feathers at the wrist of the female (below). —WILL SOOTER

MOLT

Over the course of a year, feathers become worn, frayed, and perhaps broken. Because feathers are dead structures (like human hair) and cannot be repaired, a growth of new feathers is essential for the restoration of optimal flight performance, insulation, and water resistance. The process of replacing feathers is called molt and occurs at a certain time of year, usually spring and summer. For the North American falcons (except the American Kestrel), plumage distinguishes juveniles from adults, so researchers can determine the age of a falcon for the first few years by plumage color and feather wear.

Like all vertebrates, raptors are bilaterally symmetrical, meaning that their left and right sides are mirror images of each other: skin, feathers, muscles, bones, and nerves match on both sides, more or less. Raptors maintain mostly equal feather structure from left to right even through the molt, and they are always fully able to fly. Many waterfowl, on the other hand, will drop all their primaries at once, leaving them grounded for a short time while new feathers grow back in. Molt is stimulated in part by photoperiod, the changing length of daylight associated with the seasons. Most falcon species complete their

FEATHER MOLT PATTERNS

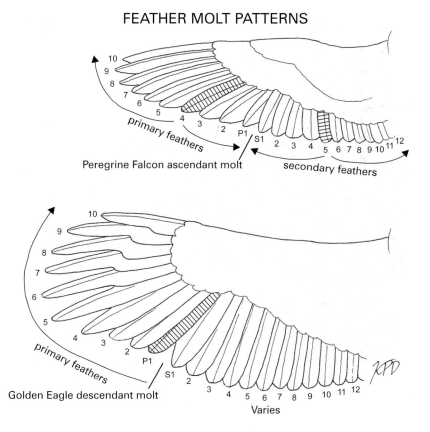

Peregrine Falcon ascendant molt

Golden Eagle descendant molt

molt by the beginning of migration in the early fall. An exception is the Tundra Peregrine, which interrupts molting to migrate, and resumes the process after arriving on its wintering ground. In falcons, both sexes start molting in the spring; the female, however, loses her feathers more quickly. She is largely sedentary, and her duties are incubating, brooding, and guarding the young. She takes advantage of this short period of relative inactivity to grow new feathers. The male supplies most of the food, and he cannot afford to be at a disadvantage when flying. His molt takes longer, continuing gradually over the spring and summer.

Feathers grow in the follicles, or small cavities in the skin, and in specific tracts called pterylae. New feathers push the old ones out. This does not occur randomly but in an orderly sequence that best allows for continued flight. Falcons have a molt pattern, called ascendant molt, that is different from that of other raptors, and it is diagnostic of the family. The primary feathers are numbered 1 through 10, starting with the inside at the wrist joint. The secondaries are numbered 1 through 12, also starting at the wrist (in the case of falcons, some birds have more or fewer). The first feather to molt is the fourth primary, with the molt continuing inward and outward. The first secondary feather to be replaced is number five. Hawks have descendant

A female Richardson's Merlin stretches. Falconers call this overhead wing stretch and tail spread a "warble." It may indicate ease and contentment.
—ROB PALMER

molt, beginning with the replacement of the innermost primary and moving outward to the wingtip. For falcons and hawks, molt is the same on left and right wing simultaneously, with the corresponding feather on each wing sometimes lost on the same day.

Tail feathers are called rectrices, and falcons have a total of twelve. Molt usually begins with the two central feathers (which falconers call "deck feathers"), with the process moving outward from there. The body is covered with contour feathers, and these also molt in predetermined sequences. Falcons have an arrangement of contour feather tracts different from that of other raptors. They also have two brood patches (areas of bare skin on the chest used for incubating eggs) instead of just one.

The relative length of the primary feathers can be used to identify large falcon species. For example, the Peregrine's number nine primary is longest, followed by the last feather, number ten. The feather formula lists relative lengths for the four longest primaries, and for the Peregrine it is 9>10>8>7 (which means primary 9 is longer than primary 10, which is longer than primary 8, which is longer than primary 7). The wing feather arrangement is different and diagnostic for the Gyrfalcon (9>8>10>7), and different still for the Prairie Falcon (9 ≥8>10 ≥7).

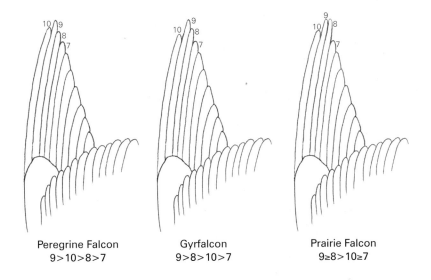

	Peregrine Falcon	Gyrfalcon	Prairie Falcon
	9>10>8>7	9>8>10>7	9≥8>10≥7

The plumage of juvenile (immature) falcons is streaked with vertical striations instead of barring, with an overall brown tinge in many species. This visible clue is a sign that they are not of breeding age and not a threat to breeding adults. This may keep the juveniles from being harassed by adults if they pass though a protected territory. The brown, striated plumage also

A male American Kestrel dives after prey. The smaller male falcons tend to be quicker in turns, aerobatics, and maneuverability than the larger females.
—ROB PALMER

helps conceal them from predators. Plus it makes them less obvious and more stealthy when hunting from perches, both bonuses for an inexperienced bird. Juvenal feathers, the first full set of flight feathers of a young bird, are less resistant to wear, partly because they grow in a short period of time. During a juvenile bird's second year, the feathers will grow over the course of about six months and will be stronger. In many larger falcon species the flight feathers of juveniles, especially tail, are longer than those of the adult. Adult plumage is attained at a year and a half and is usually identical between the sexes. Merlins and American Kestrels are exceptions, with the males being more colorful than the females.

For American Kestrels, the juvenal plumage is the same as the adult of that sex, which is atypical for raptors and unique among kestrels worldwide. In most other falcons, the juveniles have plumage comparable to the adult female for the first year. In their second year the males molt into a sex-specific plumage of their own. But for American Kestrels, the sex can be determined when their first feathers begin to grow. This species is thought to be the most recently evolved of all of the kestrels. One interesting and unusual trait of young Aplomado Falcons is that the color of their natal down is exactly that of the adult plumage.

OTHER CHARACTERISTICS

Falcons have less obvious traits that set them apart from the hawks in the family Accipitridae. Falcon eggshells are a reddish yellow on the inside, which can be seen when they are held up to a strong light. Hawk eggshells have a greenish translucence. The chemical composition of falcon eggshells is different, too, and vacuoles (small membrane-lined cavities) are absent from the outer layers. Falcons also have different feather parasites than hawks—lice of the order Mallophaga. These ectoparasites are host-specific, with different species infesting different orders of birds.

Falcons have extra tail support, with an additional pair of vertebrae fused to their pygostyle, or tailbone. These extra bones provide a greater surface area for attachment of enlarged muscles associated with the birds' high maneuverability in flight. They are able to pull out of a stoop, turn, and brake in a short distance and at high speed.

The nasal glands of falcons are also unique in shape and location. These salt-secreting glands are round and are found in the orbit (eye socket) and sinus. Those of hawks are long and thin, located in the orbit only. The nasal glands remove salt from the body fluids and excrete sodium chloride. In hawks, this fluid is seen to drip out of the nostrils and is flicked away with a quick shake of the head. Falcons instead sneeze this fluid away in a fine mist. Fluids, either nasal or salivary, or both, are fed to the young as they run down the female's beak and into the food. This may aid digestion or augment nutritional requirements.

Young falcons will hiss and *kaak* at an intruder to the nest, and adults often hiss when threatened. Whereas an excited hawk will wag its tail back and forth, a falcon bobs its tail up and down. Finally, hawks lift their tails high and eject wastes away at an angle, whereas adult falcons defecate more or less straight down (youngsters squirt wastes away from the nest). These wastes are highly concentrated in uric acid, 3,000 times stronger than the level in their blood, and are able to etch steel. While these facts may not be helpful for field identification, they nonetheless set falcons apart from other raptors. Falcons are truly a unique family of birds, perfectly adapted to the predatory lifestyle that has made them so successful worldwide.

Hovering is an energy-costly hunting strategy, but it may pay off for this male American Kestrel searching for rodents. —ROB PALMER

—2—

Falcon Behavior and Feeding

The one fact that both laypeople and scientists seem to know about falcons is that they are fast. Falcons may reach the highest speeds in the animal world, and Peregrine Falcons are the fastest. Their prey could be a bird on the wing, spotted from high above at a distance of over a mile. After some rapid wing beats, Peregrines will start a steep-angled, close-winged dive—usually less than 90 degrees but occasionally vertical. The actual speed of a Peregrine in this stoop, or dive, has been debated. A 1975 study by D. A. Orton speculated on the speed a Peregrine could achieve, taking into account the bird's size and shape. He concluded that terminal velocity—roughly, the maximum downward speed attainable—should be 227 to 237 miles per hour (365 to 381 km/h) depending on weight and drag, often minimized by body position. Vance Tucker and others found that falcons accelerate at steeper dive angles and check speed with slight head, leg, and wing adjustments. Realistic air speeds are still impressive—probably above 200 miles per hour (320 km/h), perhaps 230 miles per hour (370 km/h).

Falcons perform hyper-streamlining, with body and wing positions to make these incredible speeds possible. To reduce drag, they elongate their bodies with wings pulled tight and wrists pushed forward. Researcher Ken Franklin calls the 200-miles-per-hour-plus position "warpdrive vacuum pack." He has observed stooping falcons firsthand by skydiving with Peregrines from 16,000 feet (5,000 meters) in altitude, with the birds passing him like he was standing still!

Peregrines and Gyrfalcons are able to handle some of the highest G-forces in nature. (G-force is a measurement of acceleration in relation to the earth's gravity.) Coming out of a stoop they can pull up to 25 Gs. This is comparable to having twenty-five times the force of gravity pushing on a body. Highly trained fighter pilots and astronauts in specialized g-suits are "only" able to handle up to 10 Gs before they black out.

In a hunting stoop, falcons hold their feet forward, side by side, or tuck them tightly under the tail. At impact the prey is hit with a closed foot or feet, or swiped with an open foot armed with talons. High-speed films have shown that this second method is typical, with the toes closed into a "fist"

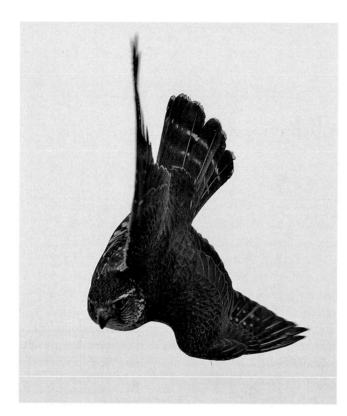

A Taiga (Boreal) Merlin's stoop. Note the three narrow light tail bands, four including the tip. —ROB PALMER

This immature Gyrfalcon has just hit a pheasant. Gyrfalcons tend to hit prey that is just flushing or on the ground, and after a "pitch up" will come in for the coup de grace, or bite to the neck. —ROB PALMER

immediately after striking. The claw on the hind toe, or hallux, is particularly effective and deadly in raking the prey. Larger prey birds are left to tumble and are often dead before they hit the ground. Peregrines and Gyrfalcons have been known to knock the heads off ducks in the sky. Smaller birds are snatched outright, or retrieved in the air after a quick turn by the falcon. Falcons are able to turn in short distances at high speed, and if the prey bird is missed the first time, they can pull up and circle back, sometimes over and over again. There seems to be a fine line between flying fast enough to catch their prey, and flying too fast and thus risking injury.

HUNTING TACTICS

American Kestrels certainly don't need to reach such high speeds to secure insects or rodents on the ground. They are often seen hovering over a hunting area scanning the terrain below—an energy-expending tactic. Hovering takes about four times more energy than level flight. Obviously, the higher they hover the more ground they can see, but the distance to the prey is increased, as is the time it takes to reach the prey, so there is a trade-off. Merlins may tail-chase a flock of birds, flying behind and selecting the one that doesn't react quickly enough or lags behind. Prey birds pack together tightly, turning in unison in an effort to confuse the falcon by presenting too many targets. An impaired bird stands out and is killed. Aplomado Falcons often employ

A Prairie Falcon takes off. —ROB PALMER

hunting tactics like those of an accipiter, crashing through brush and hopping through tight limbs in pursuit of prey. Although experts in aerial chase, many falcon species prefer eating mammals at certain times of the year. Gyrfalcons eat lemmings or ground squirrels; Prairie Falcons also prey on squirrels in spring and early summer. Peregrines will eat bats, or steal mammals such as chipmunks and squirrels from other raptors.

Although the hunting stoop is very impressive, level flight speeds aren't that fast for falcons. Studies on Merlins in unstressed, migratory flight found the average speed to be 24 miles per hour (39 km/h). Peregrines averaged 27 miles per hour (43 km/h). The record holders for air speed in level flight are members of the Apodidae family (swifts), specifically the White-throated Needletail, which is reported to reach 106 miles per hour (171 km/h) in flapping flight! These birds have long, narrow wings built for speed, similar to those of falcons.

Falcons also use a tactic that has been employed by pilots in wartime—using the element of surprise by coming straight out of bright light. Flying high with the glare of the sun at their backs, falcons are often able to approach prey without being detected until the last instant before striking.

A male Peregrine creates panic for a huge flock of blackbirds. This falcon came in in low and fast, grabbing a bird without the others noticing. Birds may resume feeding right after an attack, seemingly not concerned by the loss of one of their members. —NICK DUNLOP

A Merlin has selected a target. Note that the falcon's head and eyes are always held in the horizontal, no matter what the angle of attack. —NICK DUNLOP

Falcons can carry prey half their own body weight, and under the right conditions they can carry birds heavier than themselves. Peregrines have been known to kill Sandhill Cranes and Canada Geese, birds that weigh up to four times more than an adult Peregrine. With prey this large falcons must feed where it falls, which could make them vulnerable to predators.

Two general hunting strategies are employed by raptors, and falcons use them both. Many researchers use the terms *searchers* and *attackers* to differentiate between these two tactics. Searchers feed on small, abundant animals that are concentrated and relatively easy to catch. The epitome of such easy pickings might be late summer fields that are alive with millions of grasshoppers. This coincides with the time when young American Kestrels are perfecting their hunting skills. Inexperienced raptors exploit huge numbers of young rodents and birds that are similarly on their own for the first time, often making easier targets. Falcons may also hunt from favorite perches, dashing out (sallying) and returning to try again if unsuccessful.

Attackers are skilled hunters and have varying strategies for catching prey species that may be larger than themselves. These raptors use high stoops and dives to ambush flocks of shorebirds and waterfowl. Attackers pursuing ground prey sneak in while maintaining a low profile, wings swooped back and held motionless. This tactic is frequently used by Prairie Falcons. The success rate for aerial pursuits is low overall, but the results elicit larger prey. A bigger meal could mean less frequent hunting forays and savings in daily energy expenditure.

Falcons, like all predators, develop a search image to detect prey. Prey can blend into the environmental background via camouflage. A falcon may learn to break this defense after it's been successful in a capture. The search image also reflects the ability to detect conspicuous prey. Peregrines on the coast sometime favor a specific ocean bird, for example. And in the Midwest, certain Peregrines were adept at killing cuckoos that flew over the forest canopy. Individual birds often fixate on just a few prey species and become skilled at catching them. These prey items will make up most of their diet.

All falcons commonly cache their food, or stash the uneaten portion to retrieve it later. The cache could be in a clump of vegetation, a crack or ledge in a rock, or the crotch of a tree. Falcons sometimes cache a freshly caught animal and continue hunting. Male and female Prairie Falcons use separate caching sites, and females frequently cache more food. Kestrels may retrieve food late in the day to provide nutrition prior to a potentially cold night. Rob Palmer observed a Merlin spending thirty minutes searching for food that was cached, and one young bird never did find a Horned Lark it had hidden

Prey can remain safe and well hidden under a blanket of snow. This American Kestrel is about to capture a mouse that has ventured out.
—ROB PALMER

earlier that day. Owls also routinely cache food because they lack a crop, the storage sac in the throat of many bird species that temporarily holds food on its way to the stomach.

Raptors can be observed in behavior that can only be interpreted as play, and falcons may spend more time at this than most birds. Leslie Brown and Dean Amadon define play as "actions which seem to reflect an exuberance of physical well-being or vitality, carried out without any immediate biological goal." For example, flying Peregrines sometimes pick up and drop articles like pinecones, lichens, moss, sticks, and even dried cow pies. One captive falcon routinely stole ball caps off spectators' heads to present in subsequent display flights. Prairie Falcons have been seen tossing a clump of cow dung up in flight with both feet and trying to catch it before it fell.

Falcons often harass other birds that pose no threat, like egrets and vultures. They have been described as driving birds ahead of them and harmlessly tapping them on the back, or forcing them to retreat to the water or cover. Certain individuals have even been seen to knock larger birds to the ground with fatal wounds, and let them lie without any attempt to feed on their quarry. Trained falcons sometimes seem to delight in a difficult chase and pass up easier game. Kestrels have been observed harassing flickers just to get them to

A Peregrine Falcon at a cache site, a place it stores uneaten food. Male falcons, such as this one, may have very orange skin, deeper in color than the female.
—NICK DUNLOP

PEREGRINES CATCHING SALMONFLIES

In June 2004, Jay Sumner, Director of the Montana Peregrine Institute, witnessed a pair of Peregrine Falcons hunting stoneflies (Plecoptera order), specifically a very large species commonly called a salmonfly, along the Blackfoot River near Missoula, Montana. He saw the female catch twenty-three salmonflies during a three-minute flight in front of the nest cliff. She flew out and caught each salmonfly in the air with her talons, transferred it to her mouth, and swallowed it whole. The male also did this and then returned to the nest after catching fourteen of them as if he were delivering food. Peregrines have been observed eating the occasional insect but had never been reported eating specifically salmonflies, and lots of them.

Stoneflies are aquatic insects, and when they emerge, they swarm the banks and take flight. The salmonfly is huge, the body as big as your pinky finger, and the females are loaded with eggs. This high-calorie food item is rich in lipids. The hatch causes quite a stir amongst those who fly-fish. Daily bulletins from local fishing shops and river guides tell where the salmonflies are hatching on a given day, as the event moves upstream.

In June 2007, Erick Greene, Professor of Biological Sciences at the University of Montana, and I got a chance to see the same behavior. A male Peregrine at a cliff near Missoula was hawking salmonflies over the Blackfoot River. Greene counted twenty-two insects caught in one bout; the average time between catches was twenty-two seconds. The male would perform little stoops on the largest insects, flying upstream and swooping up and underneath. We also saw the female capture them like a flycatcher, dashing out and returning to the same rock over a dozen times.

The following day the hatch and feeding bout began at 11 a.m., and we watched the salmonfly hunting continue for several hours. The male Peregrine got to heights of over 400 feet (120 meters), and we counted fifty-one captures in one flight. Two other Peregrines, two Red-tailed Hawks, and an American Kestrel joined in the feast. Even at a distance we could see the telltale upward swoop and hunching over that meant success. The birds and bugs continued to move upstream until they were all out of sight.

Two days later I observed a pair of Peregrines catching salmonflies farther upstream at the same nest site where Sumner had seen this behavior in 2004. It may have been the same pair or an offspring with a taste for salmonflies.

A Peregrine stoops on a salmonfly hundreds of feet over the river.
—KATE DAVIS

The falcon transfers it to his mouth.
—KATE DAVIS

Note the insect wings reflecting sunlight.
—KATE DAVIS

fly. Young falcons frequently attack inanimate objects, like clumps of grass, and chase siblings around the nest site. These behaviors certainly increase their foot and flight dexterity and coordination, important skills for survival. Joel Pagel has observed Peregrines engaged in displacement behavior; instead of attacking a helicopter flying close to their nest, they often would attack passing Red-tailed Hawks and Turkey Vultures to visibly display their irritation.

FOOD

Meat is an easy food to digest. Vegetable matter requires grinding to break down the cellulose of the cell walls; a large muscular gizzard is essential for birds that specialize in plant material. Raptors have digestive tracts that are less muscular than birds with large gizzards, which reduces weight to make the birds lighter and more agile in the air. Falcon body mass is further reduced with a decrease in the size of the digestive tract; the falcon small intestine is half the length of that of the other diurnal raptors. Many falcons routinely eat small stones that falconers call "rangle," which is believed to break down the food in ways comparable to gizzards in plant-eating birds. Falcons regurgitate the stones, which may also clean the stomach and crop lining.

A falcon that isn't hungry has a different physical appearance and silhouette than one that is looking for a meal. A bulge of food at the throat indicates a full crop, and posture, preening, and other behaviors indicate to other

A female Richardson's Merlin with a songbird. —ROB PALMER

A young female Peregrine Falcon chases shorebirds in California. —NICK DUNLOP

birds that it is satiated. Prey birds may keep feeding if a nearby raptor looks uninterested. This can work to the falcon's advantage in a surprise attack. Merlins have been seen to fly in an unhurried, undulating style imitating a woodpecker, getting close to a flock before pouring on the speed for the kill. A pair of Prairie Falcons was observed to prey upon ground squirrels by apparently imitating the flight pattern of a Loggerhead Shrike, a species that poses no threat to squirrels.

Falcons have also been observed using humans to get close to game. An Aplomado Falcon used a moving train as cover, dashing from side to side after prey. A Prairie Falcon made a stealthy attack on a ground squirrel colony by flying beside an automobile to hide its approach. When close, the bird shot out across the front of the car to the other side of the road for a successful attack. A Merlin maneuvered through rush-hour traffic and an intersection, causing an unwary flock of Bohemian Waxwings to practically explode. Urban Peregrines often dart around buildings and bridges with ease and have been known to hunt at night, using streetlights and other city lights to help them see in the dark.

Prey too large to carry off easily can be stolen by raptors, even other falcons. Eagles can rob large falcons of their meals, often killing the bird in the process. These thieves or pirates are called kleptoparasites, and it is a common behavior in most raptors. In the open country habitat of a falcon, hunter and prey are visible for long distances. Hiding is difficult or impossible. Raptors mantle, or cover, their prey when feeding, hunched over with wings and tail spread. Mantling posture alone might be a cue to the kleptoparasite that the

A Merlin in a stoop. Note the four tail bands of a Richardson's subspecies, plus the white tips. The bands of a Richardson's Merlin tend to be wider than those of a Boreal Merlin. —ROB PALMER

falcon has food. Prey dangling underneath in flight is an obvious indicator. Perhaps as a defense, American Kestrels have false eyes, or ocelli, on the backs of their heads. These round spots could fool the kleptoparasite into thinking the falcon is looking right at them, thwarting any potential surprise.

Falcons are pursued by smaller birds. Songbirds routinely mob raptors and loudly protest their presence. They do this singly or in groups at target raptors perched or in flight. With loud, specific calls, the songbirds surround and dive-bomb the offending raptor and may even make contact with it. From hummingbirds to crows and ravens, mobbing birds are often smaller and more maneuverable, and they usually are not caught. These aggressive behaviors protect the flock and alert other birds to the potential danger. Bird-watchers cue on the mobbing calls and can be delighted to find a falcon at the site of such harassment.

On the other hand, a Merlin will do the same to other raptors, mobbing and chasing them to defend its personal space year-round. The untrained observer could think that they are seeing a mother and offspring, when it is actually a Merlin pestering a Golden Eagle in the dead of winter. The authors of *Hawks in Flight*, Dunne, Sibley, and Sutton, have as a rule of thumb: "If a bird passes a perched raptor and doesn't take a shot at it, then it isn't a Merlin."

Aggression between falcon species. The American Kestrel *(on the left)* became upset *when the* Merlin *(on the right)* landed on the kestrel's favorite perch. —NICK DUNLOP

PLUCKING POSTS AND PELLETS

Falcons often have a favorite plucking post, butcher block, or perch on which they de-feather and disarticulate their meal. Evidence in the field of such favored perches could include a pile of feathers, maybe discarded feet and wings, and perhaps a head. During the breeding season, parent falcons often pluck prey before taking it back to the nest. Males may pluck and eat a selected portion before presenting the rest to the female. Falcons frequently leave the head and wings intact on the carcass, with the rest of the bones stripped bare.

Raptors swallow chunks of their prey quickly, and when they close their mouth, the palate, or roof of the mouth, moves backward. The food is pushed by backward-facing spines in the throat and on the tongue called papillae. From the esophagus, food enters a temporary storage sac called the crop. When eating, hawks and falcons stretch their head up, over to one side, then back down. This motion is what falconers call "putting over," as the bird is pushing food further along to the glandular stomach, or proventriculus. The crop is elastic and can stretch to hold large amounts of food. The bulge of a swollen crop is visible just to the right side of the windpipe, or trachea. With only saliva present in the crop, little digestion of the prey takes place until it reaches the stomach.

Other evidence of a raptor in the field is the presence of pellets or boluses, which are the regurgitated remains of a meal. Falconers call them "castings."

Feathers fly after a Peregrine Falcon kills a duck. With such a large quarry, the falcon may choose to eat just the breast, leaving behind the carcass with wings still attached. —KATE DAVIS

This Merlin used the same tree near a dairy to launch attacks and eat the prey. Raptors often have a favorite plucking post, evident from feathers, feet, and wings scattered below it. —NICK DUNLOP

The carcass of a coot has been stripped clean, perhaps by a falcon. —KATE DAVIS

Raptors swallow the prey whole, or dismember it. They eat not just the meat, but also bones, feathers, fur, or the chitinous material that makes up the exoskeleton of an insect. They might pick up rocks or grass from their surroundings as well. The sorting out of what is digestible and what is not takes place in the muscular second stomach, the ventriculus, or gizzard. Members of the order Falconiformes have powerful digestive juices and can digest bones fairly well, but not structures made of keratin, such as the feathers, beaks, and claws. Strigiformes (owls) cannot digest bones or keratinous structures, so an owl's pellet contains the entire skeleton of its prey.

Undigestible material does not pass farther into the intestine, and it is compressed with muscular contractions in the gizzard. For hawks and falcons, the pellet contains some bone fragments and teeth, claws, and beaks. This makes up about 6 percent of the total composition. The pellet is covered in feathers or fur and slickened with mucus when disgorged. These little elongated balls are coughed up the day following the meal, usually in the morning, to reduce overall weight before hunting. Disgorging a pellet is semivoluntary. A bird can be seen bent over, shaking its head a few times, and out the pellet will fall. Pellets can be found below favorite roosts and nests, and when collected and dissected, can provide researchers a great deal of information about a raptor's diet. Often thought of as just a raptor behavior, scientists now know that at least 330 species of birds in sixty families worldwide produce pellets. Certain mammals, reptiles, and amphibians similarly disgorge pellets.

UPKEEP

Falcons spend considerable time each day in feather upkeep, or preening. This behavior can mean survival to a raptor that relies on precise flight and speed. All birds have a uropygial, or preen, gland at their rump at the dorsal base of the tail. This oil gland secretes waxes, fatty acids, fat, and water that the falcon applies to all of its feathers with its beak. The oil helps in waterproofing and overall insulation, and prevents the feathers from becoming brittle. By running their beaks down the length of the feathers, birds also "zip up" ones in disarray, restoring a continuous flat surface. Preening also dislodges feather parasites and cuts down on fungal and bacterial ailments. When feathers are growing, they are covered in thin sheaths, which, like the feathers themselves, are made of keratin. During molt and when young birds are growing their first feathers, these sheaths are removed by preening. The paperlike flakes and fragments are left behind or may be seen blowing in the wind.

Allopreening is the act of one bird, a mate or sibling, preening another bird's plumage. It is performed by many bird species, falcons included, and especially by owls. Falcons also bathe, dipping into shallow water or wet grass, or flying through moist foliage. As inhabitants of dry country, Prairie

Preening feathers is time-consuming and essential. These young Prairie Falcons must preen out the sheaths of feathers as they grow in. During preening, down will fly off the cliff, a visual clue that can help an observer locate a nest site. —ROB PALMER

and Aplomado falcons are more likely to dust bathe. A bout of preening or a bath is always followed by what falconers call a "rouse." For this, muscles raise the feathers, the bird shakes to realign them, and the muscles depress to lay the feathers back down. A rouse may also follow a period of rest or precede a flight. Falcons also run their faces across feathers on their back and upper wings to clean off the eye surfaces.

Hygiene is a necessity; after feeding raptors clean, or feak, their beak. They rub their beak, each side up and down and back and forth, on a limb or rock, wherever they are standing at the time. Falcons often follow feaking with other hygienic behaviors, rotating in place, kneading their feet on the substrate, and lifting their feet to nibble on toes. Another behavior, called "beaking," occurs when a nest mate "nibbles at the beak and lore area of its sibling," as Steve Sherrod described it in *Behavior of Fledgling Peregrines*. He also describes them yawning, or gaping, repeatedly for up to ten minutes. He suggests that it may be because preened down feathers are caught in their

A young Peregrine in a rouse after a meal. —NICK DUNLOP

A female Peregrine bathes in a freshwater stream where it empties into the ocean. —WILL SOOTER

*A newly fledged Merlin
yawns, or gapes. The
down on the top of the
head and very tip of the
tail is the last to be lost.*
—ROB PALMER

throat. Or perhaps this gaping equalizes pressure in their ears after a large change in altitude (like humans in airplanes) or "sudden changes in barometric pressure, as when a cold front moves in." Gyrfalcons have also been seen engaging in this behavior.

REVERSE SEXUAL SIZE DIMORPHISM

In most other vertebrates and many bird species, the males are nearly the same size as the females or slightly larger. But for nearly all raptor species, there is a noticeable size difference between the sexes, with the females being larger. This is called reverse sexual size dimorphism (RSSD). It may have evolved in unrelated bird groups, such as hawks, owls, and some seabirds, due to similar feeding, hunting, or parenting habits.

The size difference is greatest for raptors that hunt birds and thus rely on aerial prowess and dexterity. Ian Newton pointed out that size dimorphism is closely related to diet. More dimorphic species tend to feed on larger prey

A female Peregrine carries her prey, a Black-necked Stilt. —BOB STEELE

species comparable to their own weight. For falcons, the biggest size difference is in the larger species: Gyrfalcon, Peregrine, Prairie, and Aplomado. The males of these falcons are roughly one-third smaller than the females and are called tiercels, or tercels in British English, from the Latin word *tertius*, or "third." (Another theory on the origin of the term comes from the ancient falconry belief that there are two females for every male falcon.) In contrast, the biggest size difference for hawks is in the smaller species: reverse dimorphism is greatest in the Sharp-shinned Hawk, an accipiter whose diet consists almost entirely of birds. The male Sharp-shinned Hawk can be half the weight of his mate.

Researchers have struggled to explain RSSD in raptors, and several hypotheses have been proposed. Perhaps the most accepted theory is that a larger female can lay a larger egg, and subsequently guard the nest and fend off predators, as most of the incubation and brooding duties fall on her.

Size difference is small for those raptors that hunt insects, slightly greater for those that rely on mammals and fish, and greatest for raptors that rely on aerial prowess and dexterity to hunt birds. Size difference can even vary within a species; sexes are closer in size in insectivorous American Kestrels than in races that feed more on rodents.

Another related hypothesis regards niche specialization (or niche partitioning), where the different-sized sexes have different prey bases, which may reduce food competition between the males and females. The smaller male catches smaller prey, which is more abundant in both numbers of species and individuals; it is also ubiquitous and close to the nest, allowing him to make frequent food deliveries for his mate and the young. Early in nesting the demands aren't as great. When the young have grown and require more food, the female resumes hunting and supplements foraging. She can catch a wider array of species, especially larger birds that may be further from the nest (and if found near the nest, not utilized by the male). The smaller size of the male relative to the female means he needs less food for himself, and less food overall in the territory for the pair.

Other explanations for RSSD suggest that the smaller male is less likely to hurt the female or the young, and more likely to give up prey to the larger female. However, male Peregrines and American Kestrels often share incubation and brooding, and male Peregrines feed the young, so the phenomenon is still open to speculation.

These young Continental Peregrine Falcons will fledge in two to three weeks.
—NICK DUNLOP

Female Gyrfalcon on a post. The males may be 65 percent the weight of the larger females, a physical trait known as reverse sexual size dimorphism. —ROB PALMER

These one-month-old female Peregrines are already larger than their father. Male falcons are roughly one-third smaller than the females. —NICK DUNLOP

Coastal Peregrines take advantage of the abundance of seabirds near their nest.
—NICK DUNLOP

Falcon Nesting and Breeding

Falcons begin and end the breeding season in a grandiose fashion, with a relatively quiet phase of several weeks in between. Spring courtship for cliff nesters involves spectacular flights and aerobatics high over the valley or forest floor, with noisy food exchanges and brazen attacks on intruders. The smaller falcons are equally intense in courtship and nest defense. The males perform exaggerated flight displays of dives, climbs, and rolls; pairs soar in tandem. Their animated vocal exchanges resonate across rock walls and seashores, grasslands and deserts, forest openings and glades. The *kek-kek-kek* call of the smaller falcon species or *kak-kak-kak* of the larger is characteristic and can reach a crescendo at the height of courtship, during nest defense, and again when the young are leaving the nest.

The nest is quiet for about a month during incubation and early brooding. The female blends in on ledges or trees, or is hidden in the nest. While the female incubates the eggs the male often makes quick, direct flights for fast food deliveries. After the eggs hatch, noisy food exchanges to the growing chicks become louder and more frequent as the nesting season progresses. Even after the young fledge, they may still chase their parents, screaming to be fed. Siblings chase each other in play to prepare for independence, checking their flight skills around the nest site. The cryptically colored chicks of cliff nesters make the rocks come alive at feeding time. Whole families of American Kestrels fly along fence lines hunting together. Sibling Merlins roost together, and female Aplomado Falcons fly to meet the male to transfer the food to the young. After the breeding season ends, the cliffs and fields are quiet once more.

Falcons don't construct their own nests. The larger species (Gyrfalcon and Peregrine and Prairie Falcons) lay two to six eggs in open areas on cliffs called eyries. The eggs rest on a bare scrape in the detritus of a ledge, pothole, or cave, or in the abandoned or stolen nest of another bird. Either sex will make a scrape or series of scrapes until one is chosen as a nest site. The falcon leans forward, putting its weight on the breast. Rotating in a circle, it rakes loose debris with its feet, making a little depression in the soil, sand, gravel, or organic matter. A Peregrine scrape is usually 7 to 9 inches (18 to 23 cm)

A pair of Gyrfalcons, a species prone to use nests built by Rough-legged Hawks, ravens, and even Golden Eagles, used this stick nest in Alaska.
—ROB PALMER

A Prairie Falcon leaves the begging youngster behind at the nest at 6 a.m. —NICK DUNLOP

in diameter and 1 to 2 inches (3 to 5 cm) deep. Smaller birds make smaller scrapes. Eggs may even be laid on bare rock, and Peregrines use concrete ledges and metal bridge structures.

The nest might have an overhang for protection from the elements and vegetation in front for concealment. This is not always the case, though, and nests are often out in the open. Wind behaves differently on large cliffs than on the ground, and sometimes the cliff itself offers protection from the elements. Joel Pagel, who has gone into several hundred eyries in California, Oregon, and Washington, describes standing on open ledges during rainstorms and remaining dry due to updrafts and squirrelly wind gusts.

The inaccessible wall of rock also offers protection from terrestrial predators such as raccoons, foxes, weasels, and coyotes. However, predation can still occur from above by ravens, Great Horned Owls, Golden Eagles, and Cooper's Hawks. Surprisingly, some successful nests are walk-ins, so called because people (and other predators) are able to access them by walking in on the ledge. Some of these eyries are successful year after year.

Although many falcons will tolerate and even acclimate to considerable human activity near a nesting cliff, disruption from above can be a serious threat. Humans can inadvertently interrupt falcon courtship and incubation, or even cause them to abandon nest sites, sometimes with a single visit at the wrong time of the year. Some falcons locate their nests near popular river recreation and camping areas, busy urban streets, or on bridges. Yet revelers, picnickers, photographers, and rock climbers who cause no harm from below can trigger nesting failure when they move above an eyrie. Throughout North America, many recreational climbing areas are closed during the critical falcon breeding months, an inconvenience that is understandable to most who enjoy the sport. Similar disruptions come from other human activities, such as logging, firefighting, bridge maintenance, and explosives.

Falcons, especially Gyrfalcons and Peregrines, may forcibly take over old stick nests used by ravens, hawks, or Golden Eagles on cliffs. Early researchers were misled into thinking that the falcons had built the nests themselves, with detailed descriptions of what materials were favored. John James Audubon in 1840 described a Gyrfalcon nest "placed on the rocks . . . composed of sticks, sea-weeds, and mosses." Other falcons nearly always take over the nests of other species. Merlins use the abandoned nests of magpies, which have a bulky overhead dome of interlacing sticks. Raven and hawk nests are favored by Aplomado Falcons. American Kestrels nest in a natural tree cavity or woodpecker hole, and often use human-made nest boxes. Numerous kestrel box programs across the continent have been successful in restoring populations decimated by the loss of trees large enough for cavities. These programs have been instrumental in researching site-specific behavior. Urban Peregrines use boxes and trays filled with pea-sized gravel placed on building

Prairie Falcon country in Wyoming. This species relies less on water for a nest cliff than the Peregrine, but river cuts offer a good choice of ledges and potholes. —ROB PALMER

ledges. Greg Septon reports that a pair of Peregrines, one hacked (brooded in captivity and released) in Illinois and one in Minnesota, found the only nest box in the state of Wisconsin, in Milwaukee, and bred successfully in 1988! Boxes have also been installed on the cooling towers of nuclear power plants. In Oregon, a nest box placed on a cooling tower was the most productive nest site in the state. Artificial structures throughout North America are used annually by falcons for nesting and roosting.

Falcons do not add material to the nest. The eggshells are either eaten by the female or trampled into the nest. Perhaps they are removed or eaten by the parents, as they are often not found in the nest of recent hatchlings of Gyrfalcons, for example. Downy feathers will line the nest as the chicks get older and flight and contour feathers replace the down. For cliff nesters, prey remains are frequently present, with bones and debris encircling the scrape or scattered throughout. Eggshells, feathers, and prey remains are all trodden and may compress to form the actual cup or substrate of the nest.

The family's droppings, or whitewash ("hawk chalk" or "mutes" in falconry terms), are ejected over the edge; the white streaks on cliffs sometimes make certain nests or perch points obvious. Some eyries of the larger falcons have been used more or less continuously for over one hundred years, with a white

A Prairie Falcon family took over this stick nest. —NICK DUNLOP

"waterfall" streaming down the rock that is visible from more than 1 mile (1.6 km) away. A Gyrfalcon nest in Greenland could be seen from nearly 2 miles (3 km) away . Mutes may be 6 inches (15 cm) thick. These nutrient-rich droppings can encourage the growth of bright lichens, which can be used by observers as an indicator of current or historic nest presence.

Some falcons are remarkably tolerant of other birds (including raptors) at the nest cliff. American Kestrels have been observed nesting on the same cliff with Prairie and Peregrine Falcons. Prairie and Peregrine Falcons will share cliffs with Golden Eagles and Red-tailed Hawks. Prairie Falcon pairs have nested very close together, even two nests stacked vertically on the same cliff, near nests of Great Horned and Barn Owls (the latter sometimes becoming food). Falcons may benefit from nesting near ravens by taking over their stick nests and sometimes eating their young. In what may be an example of two tolerant females, one Peregrine male on the California coast successfully raised young in two nests on the same cliff in the same year!

PHILOPATRY AND COURTSHIP

Falcons exhibit *philopatry*, a term that comes from ancient Greek and means "love of the fatherland." Young falcons often return in spring to breed in the region where they fledged. *Region* is a rather vague word, but it implies a general locality and not a broad geographic area. Nest site fidelity refers to the habit of returning to the same nest in successive years. This typically involves adult birds, but it can occur with young who return to the family nest. These behavioral traits were part of the strategy researchers used for Peregrine Falcon reintroduction efforts throughout North America, with ideal habitats, cliffs, and historic eyries being chosen for nest sites. If they survived hacking and their first year, captive-bred young tended to come back to the general area where they were released—regions that afforded a good survival rate.

For American Kestrels, Merlins, Gyrfalcons, and some Peregrines, the male tends to return to the breeding grounds first and reestablish the territory. Female Prairie and Peregrine Falcons often precede the males, but this can vary with individual pairs and environmental factors at the nest site such as elevation, latitude, and aspect (which direction a nest faces). Aplomado Falcons of both sexes explore nest sites or platforms together during courtship.

The female begs and the male preens during courtship between American Kestrels. —ROB PALMER

Photoperiod, or the seasonal changes in the amount of daylight, induces physiological changes that start courtship and breeding. Falcons undergo hormonal changes that cause the male to direct his energies toward courtship. With rising hormone levels, his courtship intensity increases, with numerous defense flights and accompanying food deliveries to the female. In response to this behavior, the female's hormone levels also increase, and she becomes more receptive to food deliveries and copulation while at the same time becoming less active in preparation for egg formation and laying. Courtship lasts from three weeks to two months. Pairs of Peregrines hunt cooperatively during the preliminary courtship period. As courtship continues, however, the male provides most of the food so the female can build up her body condition. She becomes mainly sedentary to conserve energy and decrease the risk of breaking the eggs developing inside her body.

Courtship behavior of falcons can be quite spectacular, with long stoops to advertise the breeding grounds. Falcons perform aerial acrobatics: vertical dives, high-speed turns, barrel rolls, terrain hugging, and loop-the-loop maneuvers. Kestrels and Merlins have displays of exaggerated and fluttering wings. Gyrfalcons, Peregrines, and Merlins rock back and forth, alternately flashing dorsal and ventral sides in flight. This dazzling air show is often followed by high-altitude soaring by one or both falcons.

Food exchanges are accompanied by elaborate bowing and clucking bouts. The male delivers prey to the female, who might meet him high above the

The male Peregrine (on the right) *brings his mate a bird during courtship.* —NICK DUNLOP

A male Peregrine relinquishes his catch to the screaming female above the cliff nest site. —NICK DUNLOP

ground, prompting an air-to-air delivery. She might flip upside down underneath him and snatch or catch the dropped food. Other falcons seen as competitors or potential usurpers are vigorously and violently driven away. Larger intruders such as Bald or Golden Eagles and hawks are escorted out of the area with bold hostility. Even nonthreatening species such as herons and vultures are dive-bombed and struck. During the nesting season a fair share of human visitors have had their scalp raked, or nearly so, even by American Kestrels.

Ecologist Joel Pagel is attacked by a particularly aggressive female Peregrine as he enters the nest to collect data and band the chicks. He was struck by this bird as many as eighty times in twenty minutes, with twenty-seven talon marks raking his back and shoulder. —JON AVERY

A Brown Pelican is escorted away from the nesting cliff by an adult Peregrine Falcon. —WILL SOOTER

R-SELECTION AND K-SELECTION

Ecologists classify organisms as either r-selected or K-selected. R-selected species (the *r* refers to the intrinsic rate of increase in population-growth equations) often experience periods of rapid population growth. Natural selection has favored the evolution of characteristics that make individuals do well when populations are growing rapidly. Alternatively, K-selected species (from the *K* in population-growth equations) live at or near the carrying capacity of the environment. Natural selection has favored characteristics that make an individual do well when populations are stable. Few organisms employ solely one strategy or the other, but rather some combination of the two to greater or lesser degrees.

In general, r-selected species are small in body size and prone to high mortality in what might be an unpredictable environment. Their breeding densities are high, many young are produced, and there are few nonbreeding birds in the population. These species are limited by such things as aberrant weather. True r-selected bird species include Red-winged Blackbirds and European Starlings, and mixed flocks often number over a million individuals. For North American raptors, American Kestrels lean toward this category. R-selected raptors breed at one year of age (or sooner) and have a relatively large number of offspring per clutch over a relatively short life.

K-selected species are large, do not reach sexual maturity for several years, and have long life spans and thus more years to produce offspring. In contrast to r-selected species, K-selected species have fewer young, but the parents invest more time and energy in them so each individual offspring has a greater probability of reaching maturity. Breeding is energetically costly, and natural selection has favored a low breeding rate per season for these birds. Large raptors have a higher survival rate, and as Ian Newton stated, "a greater immunity from predation." Larger raptors, with their comparatively abundant stored energy reserves also survive shortages of food and harsh weather better than smaller birds. Populations of K-selected organisms are maintained at what the environment can support and are also limited by the territoriality of existing breeders.

The Golden Eagle is an example of a K-selected raptor; its productivity is limited to one or two young per year for up to twenty years. To a lesser degree Gyrfalcons and Peregrines are in this category. Populations tend to produce enough young each year to replace adults that are lost, which is called the recruitment standard. It is the lowest average brood size at which the population can maintain its numbers. Productivity below this will lead

A young female white Gyrfalcon.
—SCOTT FRANCIS

to a decline in numbers. So in a stable population, reproduction balances mortality: high reproductive rates are associated with high mortality rates. For studies with known productivity and mortality figures, population viability can be precisely determined, which could benefit conservation efforts for a species.

BREEDING

Although the larger falcons appear to have long-term pair bonds, if one is killed the survivor may acquire another mate—right away, that season, or even that day. Tom French wrote, "Peregrines mate for life, but they don't mourn for a minute." There is a population of breeding-age adults that take advantage of such losses; these individuals are called floaters. Floaters are not territorial and thus do not expend energy in nest defense. However, they can be killed or injured during interactions with breeders, or be forced into poorer quality territories as they await the chance to replace individuals at prime sites. By contrast, nonbreeders—both young and old—may inconspicuously live in or near established territories, although they more frequently live in areas without nest sites.

American Kestrels copulate after a food delivery of a mouse. Mating may occur over four hundred times for one clutch of eggs. —ROB PALMER

Once the pair bond has been established, the actual copulatory cloacal kiss occurs on a perch near the chosen nest site. It lasts just a matter of seconds, as each bird moves its tail to the side and their cloacae touch. (Birds have just one urinogenital opening, the cloaca.) For raptors this can appear awkward, as the male will ball up his feet so that his talons don't harm the female while he briefly perches on her back. Frequency and duration of copulations increase about a week before the eggs are laid, but it will continue even after the clutch is complete. Brian Walton has observed Peregrines copulating every month of the year in California. The number of cloacal kisses may reach the extreme for the American Kestrel. In one study a pair was observed to copulate 450 times per season, another pair 690 times! The male may be ensuring that it is indeed his offspring in which he is investing all of that time and energy, and not the young of an intruder that could venture in while he is out hunting for the female. Extra-pair copulations do occur with raptors, but to what extent has not been determined.

EGGS AND YOUNG

Derek Ratcliffe wrote that the eggs of the Peregrine "are among the most handsome laid by any species of bird." This holds true for all *Falco* eggs, which are a deep, rich reddish brown. The base color (the color of the egg itself, sometimes called ground color) is cream; this is then mottled, speckled, and splashed with colors ranging from brick red to rust and pink. Ratcliffe wrote that freshly laid eggs are bright and rich with "a kind of bloom." Falcon eggs are described as oval, short oval, and long oval. One end is slightly tapered so that the egg will roll in a circle and not off a cliff edge. In contrast, owl eggs are rounder, as they are usually laid in a cavity with no danger of rolling out; they are also white and lack the cryptic tint and spots that disguise falcon eggs.

Falcons lay large eggs in proportion to their body size, each egg being 10 percent of the body weight of the female kestrel. Larger raptors lay proportionately smaller eggs, which could be due to their slower metabolism. Large raptors take longer to digest food, convert it to metabolic fat and energy, and ultimately make eggs. Larger raptors also have longer intervals between eggs as they are laid, and the young take longer periods of time to grow and fledge.

Brood patches, or incubation patches, are areas on a bird's abdomen devoid of feathers. They are used for incubating eggs and keeping the young warm. Falcons have two of these patches side by side, except for American Kestrels, which have three; other raptors have just one. Hormone levels during breeding induce thicker skin with increased blood vessels at the area of the brood patch. An adult bird's body temperature is around 104 degrees Fahrenheit (40 degrees Celsius); this heat is transferred from the adult to the eggs and

The freshly laid Peregrine eggs on this scrape are the typical color of falcon eggs—a rich reddish brown. —JOEL PAGEL

young nestlings via direct contact with the brood patches. For falcons, both sexes develop brood patches in the spring, but they form later and are smaller in the males. Generally, the female does most of the incubating, with the male taking over for short spells during the day. But some individual males are more diligent in nest duties. (Also, endocrine disruption caused by persistent contaminants in the environment has been thought to affect male falcon behavior, and potentially induce feminization of males.) In extreme heat, parent falcons will incubate and brood with their back feathers raised and wings drooped to provide shade for their young. Brutal heat can be just as deadly as the cold, and eggs and nestlings can quickly die if parental duties are disrupted. Kestrel nest boxes must have ventilation to prevent overheating.

The interval between laying each egg is usually twenty-four to forty-eight hours, and incubation may begin at the third egg or when the clutch is complete. For this reason, most falcons have a synchronous hatch, with all eggs hatching more or less at once. However, falcons nesting at higher elevations and latitudes often begin incubation with the first egg due to potential freezing conditions. These birds have an asynchronous hatch, with the eggs hatching in the order they were laid and incubated. Curiously, Gyrfalcons have left eggs unattended for hours in freezing conditions without killing the developing chicks. Smaller raptors have proportionately larger eggs, more eggs per clutch, and shorter intervals between laying each egg than do large falcons. Smaller falcons also have shorter incubation times and their young reach maturity quicker. Kestrel eggs hatch on average at twenty-nine days, while the eggs of the largest falcons hatch at thirty-five days.

The actual hatching may be a relatively long process. The chick's body contracts, causing it to briefly and repeatedly straighten out. An egg tooth punctures the air sac inside the egg and chips a small hole in the shell (a process called piping). The egg tooth is a little protuberance near the end of the upper beak, which may be retained for up to a week after hatching. The chick may rest for a day in the egg as its lungs become fully functional. The chick then rotates inside the shell. Most falcons have small vestigial claws on the tips of the alulae and, for some, on the manus. These claws help the chick move about inside the shell, all the while chipping its way out with the egg tooth. Birds of prey may take thirty to seventy hours to emerge from the egg, with an average of about fifty hours total.

Falcon chicks are semialtricial, which means they are not fully developed when they hatch and are dependent on their parents for food and care. Unlike fully altricial chicks, which have no feathers when they hatch, falcon chicks

A newly hatched Peregrine chick still has its egg tooth (and eggshell). —ROB PALMER

are covered with a thick layer of white down. Their eyes are closed or barely open as slits; they fully open at one to five days. Hatchlings cannot maintain their own body temperature, or themoregulate, for the first few weeks, so they must be brooded almost constantly by one of the parents. In some falcons, the male will brood the young to let the female feed, bathe, and defecate.

The young are nidicolous, meaning they remain in the nest and are fed by the parents. The young, also called eyases, are fed by the female for the first few weeks. The female presents little strips of meat to the beak of the hungry eyases. She will make a soft *chip* or *chup* sound and touch their beaks to entice the chicks to open their mouths. After their eyes are open, movement will bring about feeding behavior. When the young are able to thermoregulate (after about two weeks), the male helps feed them in the nest. Parents continue to present little morsels to the young even after they are able tear up food themselves. In most falcons, however, the female does the majority of the feeding of eyases after receiving prey, often already plucked, from the male. Later in the nesting, the adults simply drop the prey at the nest and let the young feed themselves.

There is often no serious aggression between falcon chicks in the nest, unlike several species of hawks and most eagles. In other raptors the offspring

A parent falcon presents little strips of meat to the youngster. This chick is pictured on page 105, two years later.
—KENNY STERNER

These Peregrine chicks are about three weeks old. —JOEL PAGEL

kill their siblings outright, with no intervention by the parents. This is called siblicide or fratricide (or Cainism as in Cain and Abel). Falcon eyases don't kill each other, although there can be disagreements about who gets what at feeding time.

Reverse sexual size dimorphism (the phenomena where the females of a species are larger than the males) might suggest the smaller male nestlings would be at a disadvantage. In Peregrines and Gyrfalcons, nestling males are roughly one-third smaller than their sisters and can be sexed by their smaller tarsus and shorter toes at about two weeks of age. To make up for their smaller size, males are behaviorally and physiologically advanced, are able to feed themselves sooner, and fledge from the nest at an earlier age.

Hazards can occur at the falcon nest. If one clutch of eggs is destroyed due to an accident, broken due to contaminant-induced eggshell thinning, or stolen by a predator (or egg collector), falcons will "recycle." This means they will go through an abbreviated courtship process to lay a second clutch of eggs, usually two to three weeks after the initial nest failure. This could put the young at a disadvantage, as they will be fledging later in the season than normal, which might be risky when a long-distance migration is to follow.

People who breed falcons and other raptors for falconry or conservation induce the birds to lay a second clutch to increase the gross number of young produced in a season. A Peregrine is able to lay twelve to sixteen eggs in one season if the eggs are taken one by one as they are produced. Breeders will often place the first eggs with a foster bird, or hatch them in a humidity-controlled incubator. But there is a trade-off for the breeder. By forcing the captive female to lay more eggs per season than normal, the overall number of years the she will lay eggs is reduced.

FLEDGING

The term *fledging* actually means "becoming feathered," but a meaning more widely used by biologists and ecologists is "leaving the nest." Falcons fledge between twenty-eight and fifty-four days, depending on species and sex. To prepare for flight, falcon young vigorously flap their wings, occasionally catching a bit of air as they practice this necessary skill. Some falcons also scramble around on the rock face near their eyrie. First flights can be comical to the human observer because while the young bird may instinctively know how to fly, it frequently will not have the muscle control to land gracefully. Newly fledged falcons often try to land with too much or too little speed, and select a

25 DAYS   29 DAYS   34 DAYS

37 DAYS   40 DAYS   45 DAYS

A captive Peregrine's growth is chronicled, from 25 days of age (at upper left) *to 45 days* (at lower right), *when its feathers are nearly fully grown.* —KATE DAVIS

tiny bush, scrawny limb, or leaf on which to settle. For the first several weeks of flight, the approximate age of a newly fledged falcon can be judged by its flying and landing style. During this time fledglings are at an increased risk of death due to accidents and predation; survivors improve quickly and hone their flight and hunting skills.

As with most raptors, first-year mortality for falcons is high. Up to 75 percent of the young may die during their first year, although 65 percent is a more generally accepted figure. Hazards occur at the nest, where the young are defenseless and concentrated in one spot. The nest can be a source of food for predators such as Great Horned Owls, Cooper's Hawks, Golden Eagles, and raccoons. In addition, extreme weather and storms affect survival. Parasites can also weaken young, causing them to die later. The extreme hunting style of falcons can also be dangerous; a falconers' joke is that a falcon learning to fly is like a sixteen-year-old human who's been given a Ferrari.

Fledged falcons rely on their parents for food from three weeks to three months, depending on species and site. Most falcons won't hunt independently for three to six weeks after fledging. Although they may not return to the nest ledge, falcons continue to use the general cliff site. Ravenous young falcons pose a minor threat to the adults, especially when the hungry

Young Peregrines await a food delivery. The bird on the right is older, with more feather growth. Unlike hawks, there is very little outright aggression between siblings in a falcon nest. —NICK DUNLOP

A young male American Kestrel peers from his nest cavity in a tree. —ROB PALMER

fledglings pursue the smaller male. Males have been observed flinging freshly killed prey to the young, or just dropping the meal and taking off.

Falcons from American Kestrels to Peregrines have been observed hunting socially in family groups after the young have fledged. Dispersal occurs when the young leave the parental territory; this can happen gradually or suddenly. The young become more independent and eventually are on their own. The term *dispersal* mainly applies to the activity of the young, but it can refer to adults as well. Dispersal is movement in any direction and may be related to food sources. Some Prairie Falcons, for example, move to separate hunting grounds in midsummer after nesting.

Young falcons must learn where to safely roost at night to avoid predators such as owls. Disease can take its toll. Human-caused accidents also lead to mortality: collisions with vehicles, power lines, mirrored windows on sky-scrapers, and aircraft take the lives of many falcons each year. Urban falcons that choose to nest on bridges are especially vulnerable because of the erratic and turbulent winds around girders and beams. Fledglings often have a nearly impossible first flight from a bridge and drowning is common. Falcons are electrocuted as they land on power poles that have bare wires and exposed transformers. The wings of larger falcons might span between two hot wires. Environmental contaminants and pesticides continue to take their toll with invention of new compounds. The most preventable mortality is by gunshot, which despite lawful protection and public education, still occurs.

Mortality rate drops to perhaps 10 to 20 percent per year as young falcons fine-tune their survival skills. Peregrines are believed to have a high after-hatch-year mortality rate of 25 to 40 precent. Large falcons may live fifteen or twenty years in the wild, but this is rare. Very few of the smaller falcons make it to ten years of age. The difficult lifestyle of a predator weeds out the birds that make mistakes and favors those most capable of surviving its intricacies.

Newly fledged Continental Peregrines, called "brownies" by falcon watchers and researchers, are fed by the parents for several weeks. —NICK DUNLOP

Male Peregrines may risk attack by voracious, noisy youngsters when delivering food.
—NICK DUNLOP

A Gyrfalcon launches into flight. —ROB PALMER

—4—

Falcon Movements

Among the most devoted participants in raptor fieldwork are the hawkwatchers. For several months a year they keep their eyes to the sky to record species and numbers of raptors passing through on migration. These highly skilled raptor enthusiasts work from ridgetops, lakeshores, and even hotel roofs. Subtle differences that make bird identification possible at a mile away come into play at a hawkwatch site. A skilled hawkwatcher can tell a Prairie Falcon from a Peregrine Falcon when it is a speck in the distance. Hawkwatchers are also able to recognize subtle differences such as sex, age, feather condition, or color morph. The data recorded by paid and volunteer observers are invaluable in assessing long-term raptor population trends in ecosystems far removed from the hawkwatch location.

MOVEMENTS

When most people think of bird travel, they think of migration—birds flying north for the summer and south for the winter. However, there are many other types of movements, such as dispersal, emigration, and nomadism. These movements occur for a variety of reasons, including food availability or competition. Natal dispersal, for example, occurs when the young become independent of their parents and move away from the nest site. Emigration strictly means to leave an area, and nomadism indicates random movements or wandering in response to local conditions. Nomadic birds may have irregular patterns of distribution.

MIGRATION

The ability to fly makes long-distance migration possible for birds, insects, and bats. Forty percent of the world's ten thousand species of birds annually move from a summer breeding ground to a nonbreeding location. Migration allows birds to exploit favorable conditions at different geographical areas at different times of the year, thus improving lifetime reproductive fitness. Of the world's raptors, 62 percent (about 183 species) migrate.

Prairie Falcons are open country birds that feed primarily on ground squirrels all summer, then switch to a diet of birds after the squirrels retreat underground. —NICK DUNLOP

A Peregrine checks out the photographer near its coastal California nest.
—NICK DUNLOP

Different migration strategies exist among different bird species. There are even differences, often dependent on sex or age, among individuals of the same species. Multiple species use one route to migrate southward and use a completely different route to migrate northward. Many migratory animals have predictable movements, some of which occur every year. Raptors also migrate altitudinally, moving to higher elevations in the summer and lower elevations in the winter. Some species migrate less than 100 miles, others thousands of miles, and one in particular, the Tundra Peregrine, flies nearly from pole to pole.

For most raptors, migration is a twice-yearly event initiated by external factors that include changes in temperature, local weather conditions, photoperiod, and the availability of food. Falcons have a full range of migration strategies and often travel the farthest of any raptor. Strategies can vary among different subspecies, depending on the latitude where they nest. For example, Peregrines that breed above the Arctic Circle regularly winter in Chile and Argentina in southern South America. This may amount to a yearly round-trip flight of up to 18,000 miles (29,000 km). As they travel six to eight weeks each way, they may cross over the political boundaries of thirteen countries. Not all migrant Peregrines travel to South America; some winter as far north as British Columbia, and there are even records of Peregrines wintering in Greenland. Others may remain in the continental United States, including Florida, Texas, the Gulf Coast, and the Pacific states at elevations of up to 4,000 feet (1,220 meters). The Peale's Peregrine of the Pacific Northwest

This Peregrine is comfortable resting on a building in San Jose, California.
—EVET LOEWEN

SOUTHERN CROSS PEREGRINE PROJECT AND FALCON RESEARCH GROUP

An ambitious project to track the migration of Peregrine Falcons was begun in 2007 by the nonprofit Falcon Research Group (FRG). Biologist and founder Bud Anderson and his fellow researchers were interested in Tundra Peregrines, who on their yearly migration rack up nearly 18,000 miles (29,000 km) round-trip. Anderson named the study the Southern Cross Peregrine Project, after the famous star constellation in the southern hemisphere. Chile was chosen as the research site because very little was known about Peregrine Falcons' wintering behavior there, or their migration distances and routes.

In February 2007, a team of five Americans, one Spaniard, and one Chilean began the fieldwork. Seven Peregrine Falcons were eventually fitted with state-of-the-art GPS trackers. The 1-ounce (30-gram) trackers, embedded with microchips, were able to produce up to three signals per day, revealing the birds' location within 60 feet (18 meters). These locations were then uploaded to a Google Earth map on the Southern Cross Web site. Bird lovers around the world watched on the Internet as tagged birds sped their way from South America to Canada. Blogs and maps posted on the FRG website reflected each bird's progress. Three team members returned to Chile in 2008 and tagged four more birds. These Peregrines led the Southern Cross researchers to some important discoveries.

Scientists had long assumed that Peregrine Falcons traveled between 100 and 120 miles per day (160 and 190 km/day) while migrating. Several birds often traveled more than 300 miles per day (480 km/day), and a male named Fireball broke all known speed records for falcons by traveling 566 miles (911 km) in one twenty-four-hour period. He crossed over a big portion of Northern Mexico, Texas, Oklahoma, and most of Kansas in just three days, a distance of 1,455 miles (2,342 km). Fireball ended his forty-five-day northern migration above the Arctic Circle on the northernmost landmass in North America, the Boothia Peninsula. Researchers found that falcons would stop to rest and feed for several days at a time, and that they would migrate at night. Another bird from the study was the first GPS-tracked Peregrine Falcon to be photographed during migration (by Costa Rican photographer Marco Saborio), the antennae clearly showing in the images.

A male called Sparrow King was tracked to and from breeding grounds on Baffin Island two years running. On his southern route, he began with an ocean crossing of 117 miles (189 km) flying across the Hudson Strait. He then followed the typical eastern route and roosted one night at Hawk Mountain Sanctuary—right next to the office of Keith Bildstein, the man responsible for purchasing his transmitter! In 2008, he took a slightly shorter route north, and returned to the same eyrie nine days sooner. These birds are astounding the scientific and birdwatching world with their migration feats. As Bud Anderson said, "Peregrines really are a perfect natural ambassador to link countries, to link continents, to link cultures, and we hope, to link classrooms."

Sparrow King, aka Sparky, an adult male Peregrine Falcon fitted with a GPS tracker, followed a clockwise loop migration route in 2007 and 2008. —MARK PROSTER

2007 Northern Migration: April 11 to June 8 (58 days); 7,992 miles (12,861 km)
2008 Northern Migration: April 18 to May 30 (42 days); 7,539 miles (12,132 km)

Coast is more sedentary, displaying shorter annual movements, with some individuals not migrating at all.

Banding records and radio telemetry studies have also shown that many Continental Peregrines move to the southern United States, Mexico, and Central and South America for the winter months. Still others reside in urban areas and, as city dwellers with ready access to an abundant food supply of pigeons and starlings, may stay put all year. For example, at least four pairs of breeding Peregrines remain throughout the winter in Seattle, Washington, at 47 degrees north latitude, and others move to Portland, Oregon, during the winter months.

The principle of varying migration strategies also holds true for Merlins, and each of the three subspecies has a different pattern. The long-distance migrants are the Boreal Merlins (*F. columbarius columbarius*). Nearly the entire population of these northern breeders winters in an area from the southern United States through Mexico and Central America to South America north of the equator. The western and central Richardson's Merlins (*F. c. richardsoni*) generally stay in the United States and travel a shorter distance during migration. Urban Richardson's Merlins are often year-round inhabitants exhibiting little movement, even those that live as far north as Canada. The West Coast Black Merlins (*F. c. suckleyi*) are thought to be sedentary (few have been banded), but some are known to move down the coast to Baja, Mexico, and some winter at inland locations in the western United States.

American Kestrels are year-round residents in Southern Canada, portions of the United States, and Mexico. The northernmost Canada and Alaska birds move the farthest south in winter; the southeastern United States subspecies (*F. sparverius paulus*) is sedentary. Male American Kestrels tend to winter closer to the breeding territories than the females.

Prairie Falcons show unique tendencies among the falcons in their seasonal migrations: instead of two trips each year (north and south), some populations make three. They travel north and east and to higher elevations after breeding, then travel south for the winter, returning to their breeding grounds in the spring—forming a clockwise, three-stop migration pattern. Karen Steenhof found individuals traveling up to 2,800 miles (4,500 km) annually. In Idaho, their mammal diet of Townsend's (Piute) Ground Squirrels becomes less available in the late summer when the squirrels retreat underground and estivate (like hibernating in summer) to avoid extreme heat. Prairie Falcons then move to the northern Great Plains and feed on Richardson's Ground Squirrels until cool temperatures induce the squirrels to hibernate. Prairie Falcons then move again, changing their hunting strategy by shifting to an avian diet. Therefore, their migration routes are governed by the availability of food.

A Prairie Falcon captures a mouse that has ventured above the snow. —ROB PALMER

An immature Gyrfalcon soars. It is usually first-year and female Gyrfalcons that make it to the lower forty-eight states in the winter. —ROB PALMER

Most adult male Gyrfalcons are thought to remain on the breeding grounds in Alaska and Canada during the cold Arctic winter. The majority of migrants observed in the continental United States are adult females and young birds of both sexes. As with Prairie Falcons, the seasonal movements of Gyrfalcons are also affected by food availability. The number and availability of prey fluctuates greatly, but these fluctuations are fairly predictable. Small rodents, including voles and lemmings, tend to have a three- or four-year population cycle, Snowshoe Hares a seven- to eleven-year cycle, and ptarmigans four- or ten-year cycles. Other northern raptors, including Goshawks, Rough-legged Hawks, and Snowy Owls, migrate and move farther south when the prey populations reach annual low points. When prey numbers periodically fall to a catastrophic low, abnormally large numbers of birds move south in what is termed an *irruption* year.

Most Northern Aplomados are sedentary and remain on their breeding territories in Texas, New Mexico, and Mexico all year. However, some practice seasonal altitudinal movements that can be in any direction. Some individuals retreat to lower elevations in the winter, and birds released in Texas roam west and north at any time of the year.

TACTICS AND STRATEGIES

Keith Bildstein succinctly describes the tasks that raptors must achieve to survive a seasonal migration. They must leave their natal area, find suitable wintering or nonbreeding territories, and then return to and select a breeding area in the spring. Their north and south migrations must correspond with "appropriate climatic and ecological conditions." And finally, the raptors should arrive at their destination in good physical condition to overwinter or breed; it is critical that they are not too weak or compromised.

Paul Kerlinger proposed three categories of migration: complete, partial, and irruptive. For complete migration, at least 90 percent of the population leaves the breeding grounds to winter elsewhere. Complete migrants in North America include Swainson's, Broad-winged, and Rough-legged Hawks and most populations of Ospreys (except those in south Florida). Partial migrants are those raptor species in which only some individuals have separate breeding and wintering grounds. All six North American falcon species are partial migrants. Breeding and nonbreeding ranges may or may not overlap for partial migrants. The third category, irruptive or local migration, is dictated by changing prey populations in a given area. In some years, birds will travel as a response to a lack of prey; in other years, they won't travel at all. Among the thirty-seven species of falcons worldwide, only seven are irruptive migrants: the Orange-breasted, Bat, Grey, Black, and Lagger Falcons, African Hobby, and Greater Kestrel.

Kerlinger used radar tracking at many locations to observe raptor migration in North America. His studies indicated that during migration 80 percent of raptors fly at altitudes of around 3,300 feet or less (1,000 meters). American Kestrels usually migrate at treetop level, and Peregrines at or below 2,950 feet (900 meters). High-altitude migration, on the other hand, may be physically stressful due to extremely cold temperatures, but may be beneficial to migrants due to favorable winds. Raptor migrants that are known to travel at elevations of nearly 16,000 feet (4,800 meters) include Turkey Vultures, Swainson's and Broad-winged Hawks, and Bald Eagles. The recent Southern Cross Peregrine Project showed that satellite-tagged Peregrines migrated through the Andes Mountains in Bolivia at 13,500 feet (4,110 meters). However, the record documented altitude of a raptor is an unfortunate Ruppell's Griffon, an Old World vulture, that was struck by an airliner 37,000 feet (11,300 meters) above the Ivory Coast of West Africa.

Many songbirds, shorebirds, and geese are nocturnal migrants, and use considerable energy in flapping flight. Since raptors only migrate during the day, nighttime migration by other birds reduces exposure to potential

Raptors like this young Peregrine are daytime migrants, "solar-powered" in the words of researcher Keith Bildstein. —NICK DUNLOP

predation by raptors. Bildstein referred to raptors as "solar-powered" soaring travelers.

Falcons prefer overland routes, although Merlins will cross water, reportedly low and close to the waves. Peregrines will also cross large expanses of open water, and some individuals have flown long distances over water and have perched on boats far out at sea. For example, K. H. Voous reported that in 1961 a Peregrine landed on a freighter that was 800 miles (1,300 km) from land in the Atlantic Ocean west of Africa. This bird stayed aboard the ship for several days and flew off when the boat was still more than 700 miles (1,100 km) from South America. To reach land at a speed of 50 miles per hour (80 km/h), it would have had to fly at least sixteen hours to reach Africa and fourteen hours to reach South America. Another adult Peregrine regularly wintered for many years in the Galápagos Islands, nearly 600 miles (970 km) from the Ecuadorean coast. But the current long-distance record for an oceanic water crossing by a Peregrine must be those seen in the winter on Maui, Hawaii. This tropical archipelago is the most remote island group in the world and is located 2,300 miles (3,700 km) from the nearest continental landmass in California. Such a crossing is remarkable enough, but it should be noted that, in 2007, a Peregrine flew aboard a cruise ship near Vancouver Island, British Columbia, Canada, and traveled all the way to Oahu on board!

In North America, autumn raptor migration begins in late August and generally lasts until mid-November. Observation and banding data show that the peak numbers are usually about two weeks earlier in the West than the East. Peregrine migration is four to six weeks earlier on the West Coast than East Coast, with intermediate peaks inland. The smaller raptors (American Kestrels) and long-distance migrants (Tundra Peregrines) tend to migrate earlier. Northern sites generally see earlier peaks than southern, as do inland versus coastal areas.

ATMOSPHERIC CONDITIONS

Raptors use thermals to gain altitude while expending less energy than they would in flapping flight. Thermals are formed when the earth's surface has been heated, and the warmer, lighter air rises. Thermals don't often form over bodies of water, so most raptors are reluctant to cross large lakes and oceans. Land surfaces absorb and reflect heat at different rates. Arid fields, asphalt parking lots, and rocks absorb heat best, with dark rocks absorbing heat especially well. Thermal lift from the rising air is strongest on sunny days from midmorning until late afternoon; by late afternoon, vertical thermals are weakened by strong disruptive horizontal winds. Cumulus clouds usually form over thermals and are indicators of favorable soaring conditions for raptors, which circle and soar where these thermals are rising fastest. During migration, raptors stream, or glide, to the next thermal on their route to repeat the process. Raptors locate thermal pockets by observing other raptors; young birds watch the experienced adults of the same or other species.

Falcons are adept at using thermals but more often migrate with an active, flapping flight. This comes with a greater metabolic cost, as it is much higher in energy use than passive, soaring flight. Paul Kerlinger estimates that soaring flight uses only a quarter of the energy of powered flight. However, direct flapping flight minimizes the time it takes to get to the winter range, since circling to gain altitude takes a great deal of time and achieves little forward advancement. Powered flight allows the falcon's forward progression to be steady and constant.

The larger falcons are able to migrate in weather conditions that ground other migrant raptors. Overcast days, high winds, rain, and snow may not hinder falcon flight. In addition, falcons can modify their high-speed wing shape to make themselves more efficient for soaring. They broaden their wings, extending them fully and creating a slotted surface on each wing with the primary feathers to create more lift. While the buteo hawks, eagles, and vultures have the most efficient wing structure for soaring, through convergent evolution falcons have adopted a similar design.

Migrating raptors also engage in slope soaring. This occurs when winds blowing horizontally across the terrain are deflected upward when they strike

The powerful wing beats of an adult Peregrine can propel these birds to speeds of 75 miles per hour (120 km/h) in level flight. —ROB PALMER

a barrier, such as a hill, mountain, line of trees, or tall buildings. Peregrines use sea cliffs to take advantage of a long line of deflection-induced updrafts. They have also been observed using the steam from power plant cooling towers to gain height.

Weather conditions may stimulate migration south and bring days of huge raptor numbers. In eastern North America, a fall cold front moving in from the north causes favorable winds for migrating raptors. The high-pressure cells following cold fronts cause increasing barometric pressure, dropping temperatures, and clearing skies for rapid seasonal changes. The day after a cold front passes in midfall is the best time to see large numbers of migrant raptors heading south. North and northeasterly winds push the birds south. The reverse often holds true in most western portions of the continent; cold fronts push birds ahead of them, and the best flights are the day before these weather systems arrive. The highest numbers of migrant Peregrines seen at Padre Island, Texas, in the fall are associated with cold fronts.

In the spring, winds flow strongly from the south. The spring migrations generally don't have the huge numbers of raptors seen during the fall migration. Mortality of first-year birds over the winter results in fewer numbers overall, and thermals occur over a wider range so birds are more dispersed as they move north.

Falcons are solitary migrants; they don't travel in huge flocks like many hawks. The exception is American Kestrels, which travel in loosely associated groups of up to ten individuals. Other falcon pairs are thought to migrate separately. However, Laurie Goodrich described Peregrines that appeared to be migrating together at Hawk Mountain, Pennsylvania, and pair behavior is often observed at Padre Island. Falcon pairs might share a wintering ground. Bud Anderson, Christian Gonzalez, and Oscar Beingolea have observed many wintering pairs, or pseudo-pairs, among migrant Peregrines in Ecuador, Peru, Chile, and Argentina. Adults perch together, hunt together, and even share kills. However, these are most likely to be social bonds developed on the wintering ground only. Copulation is not a feature of these pairs.

Many raptors, including falcons, engage in ecological leapfrog migration. High latitude or upper elevation populations leave their breeding grounds and travel farther south than birds at lower latitudes. Far northern Peregrines generally fly farther south than Continental and Peale's Peregrines, leapfrogging over the more sedentary subspecies. Washington, Oregon, and northern California Continental Peregrines may also exhibit leapfrog migration to lower elevations and more southerly latitudes. American Kestrel males tend to winter farther south than females; the northern-latitude kestrels pass over the winter and year-round resident territories already held by southern birds. Northernmost falcons begin their fall migration earlier than southern latitude birds; their breeding season is shortened at high latitudes. Falcons are

A Peregrine Falcon launches into flight.
—NICK DUNLOP

highly territorial on the breeding grounds, and many also exhibit this behavior toward migrants over the fall and winter.

Many raptors exhibit loop or elliptical migration, having different departure and return migration routes. Numbers at migration count sites are often vastly different between fall and spring as a result. In the northern hemisphere, loop migrations tend to be clockwise in direction, due largely to prevailing winds at different times of the year. Not necessarily all of the individuals in a population practice this, but it is seen in northern Peregrines, for example. Birds radio marked in the far north journeyed south along the east coast of the United States to Central and South America, and headed back north though the central United States, thereby following a large elliptical path.

PREPARATION

In order to prepare for migration, most raptors (Swainson's and Broad-winged Hawks, for example) engage in hyperphagia, or excessive eating, which can increase their body mass by up to 20 percent. Some falcons increase their body mass in the summer; American Kestrels do so by as much as 4 percent.

However, recent studies suggest that Peregrines actually lose a lot of weight over the breeding season while feeding themselves and the young, so some of this gain may be making up for lost weight.

Falcons feed during migration, adapting to what is available along the way. American Kestrels pass over areas that provide poor hunting opportunities (deep forest) and linger in open country to feed. Falcons will also take advantage of abundant prey along the way. For example, migrating Merlins and American Kestrels have been observed feeding on swarming insects. Peregrines have stopover sites and will halt migration for several days or weeks to opportunistically hunt migrating songbirds, waterbirds, and shorebirds that have congregated at these spots. Migrating raptors will also stop and wait out a bout of especially bad weather along the way. Through satellite telemetry, the Southern Cross Peregrine Project (see pages 80–81) determined that a day or two of rest often follows a particularly long migration day.

Molt is a mechanism to replace worn feathers, and some migrant raptors stop molting until they reach their winter destination (the Tundra Peregrine

American Kestrels will feed on swarms of crickets, grasshoppers, and other insects en route during migration. —NICK DUNLOP

This Peregrine Falcon stooped on a flock of shorebirds, vigorously chasing birds that broke away from the flock. —NICK DUNLOP

is a good example). Migration is a critical aspect of the raptor's life history, and individuals greatly benefit from their feathers being in top shape. Gaps of lost feathers in the wings and tail would dramatically reduce their ability to fly. For American Kestrels, completion of the feather molt is a migration trigger. Female American Kestrels complete their molt and leave the breeding grounds first, along with young birds with their newly grown feathers. Merlins may also time migration by their molt, rather than by factors such as photoperiod, weather, and prey availability.

NAVIGATION

Avian navigation over vast distances and between continents has long fascinated researchers. How do birds move across terrain, constantly reorienting themselves in all sorts of weather, to reach a traditional wintering habitat? How does this occur when a young bird has never made the trip before? Falcons exhibit a high degree of winter philopatry; for example, Tundra Peregrines are known to return to the exact same perches in South America winter after winter. Cues from the environment are partial guides, such as bodies of water, vegetation, and open country, in addition to the sun, stars, and the earth's magnetic field. Birds also recognize and use regional and local landmarks and topographical features. Often they will follow leading lines in the direction of travel, such as mountain ranges and coastlines, and take

Peregrine Falcons may rest for a day after a particularly long or difficult session of migration. They may also sit out bouts of bad weather. —ROB PALMER

advantage of mountain passes and ridges and narrow coastal plains. Falcons especially will also follow flocks of migrating shorebirds, and individual Merlins and Peregrines will follow coastlines.

Padre Island, Texas, is a migration hotspot for many North American Peregrines. Huge numbers of continental and tundra birds pass along this coastal barrier island before heading south along the Gulf of Mexico. Almost 700 were banded there in a single fall. Others stay inland, flying overland through Mexico. The Florida Keys site called Curry Hammock has probably the highest daily (521 is the record) and yearly Peregrine numbers, with 2,858 passing through in one season. Cape May, New Jersey, counted 298 Peregrines on one October 2001 day, and the high daily count for Kiptopeke State Park on the coast of Virginia was 364 Peregrines on an October day in 1997. Incidentally, Kiptopeke also had 462 Merlins on one day in 1998.

Birds that have somehow been blown off their normal migration route can cause quite a stir in the birdwatching world. Reports of these sightings are maintained by the Hawk Migration Association of North America (HMANA). The early Peterson Field Guides called them "accidentals" and the "rarest of the rarities." Eurasian Kestrels might be casual visitors to the east and west coasts of North America. Individuals have been reported from the Aleutian Islands south to British Columbia, Washington, and California. Eurasian Hobbies occasionally arrive in the Aleutian Island region, and one was sighted in Seattle, Washington, in October 2001. A single Collared Forest-Falcon made it to Texas in 1994. And thousands of birders made a trek to Martha's Vineyard on the Massachusetts coast in August of 2004 for a glimpse of a Red-footed Falcon, which normally breeds in Eastern Europe and central Asia and winters in Africa.

HAWKWATCHING

Raptors have been migrating at least 40 million years. Our human ancestors were likely to have had an interest in these movements for a variety of reasons. Our knowledge of the relationships between humans and raptors dates to about six thousand years ago, when raptors were trapped for food, then trained for falconry, later shot for sport, and currently counted for science. These migration counts have become essential for research into population dynamics and trends.

Thousands of nestling, migrant, and wintering raptors are now captured each year in North America and banded with individually numbered aluminum bands on their legs, then released unharmed. The U.S. Geological Survey Bird Banding Laboratory coordinates the effort and provides the aluminum leg bands. Even with the low return rate (less than 1 to 5 percent of all banded birds), important geographical and life history data are collected about each bird during banding. At most raptor banding stations, morphological measurements are usually taken on each bird, and their feather molt, fat content, and general condition are noted. Banding stations are critical to the study of migrating raptors, as are the people—usually volunteers—who do the work.

Raptors are also fit with visual identification (VID) bands that have different colors and codes. Some individual birds are marked with lightweight wing tags (patagial markers). Much of our detailed information on migration has been collected through radiotelemetry. In the early 1980s satellite telemetry for raptors was developed and is now providing astounding results. A transmitter, traditionally weighing less than 3 percent of the body mass of the raptor, is placed on a bird as a backpack and emits a signal picked up by a satellite. Satellite tracking results in accurate details of raptor movements, even down to the precise location of night perches or roosts. Recent developments in global positioning systems (GPS), solar-powered satellite transmitters, and earth imaging software such as Google Earth have revolutionized the field. It is now possible to locate marked birds within approximately 60 feet (18 meters) anywhere on earth. Although about $3,000 to $4,000 per unit, the costs are decreasing and transmitters are getting smaller. As a result, raptor field research is expanding significantly and entering realms we could have only dreamed of a decade ago. Scientists can now track birds across the planet, hour by hour, and follow them on a long-term basis. Bildstein has accurately called satellite telemetry the "holy grail" of the new migration technology.

Another new development with huge potential is the analysis of stable isotopes. Many elements have different numbers of neutrons in the nucleus, and each variant is called an isotope. A North American map of stable hydrogen isotopes, measured from collected precipitation, was made by Casey Lott and Jeff Smith of HawkWatch International. Hydrogen isotopes varied according to latitude and elevation in broad bands. Animal tissue contains signature stable isotopes related to diet, and analysis of that tissue indicates

 COASTAL RAPTOR MONITORING

Falcons on the Washington coast might recognize the Isuzu Trooper full of researchers cruising the beach from year to year. Since 1995, Dan Varland and his crew from the Coastal Raptor Monitoring program have been combing three beaches in a study area southwest of Seattle. Peregrines are the primary target species for capture and banding, but the researchers also band Merlins, Gyrfalcons, and Bald Eagles in hopes of understanding more about raptor biology.

Surveys are regularly conducted from September through May, with some occasional summer monitoring. Transects are driven starting just before sunrise. All captured birds are quickly measured, weighed, and photographed. Feathers are collected for a procedure known as stable isotope analysis. Blood samples are taken from Peregrine Falcons to test for contaminants and determine subspecies. A metal color band is secured to one leg according to the falcon's subspecies. Green color bands are placed on Peale's Peregrines. Combination black and blue bands are used on the Continental and Tundra subspecies, and on individuals that cannot safely be identified to subspecies in the field. A U.S. Fish and Wildlife Service band is then placed on the other leg. These bands are colored according to the beach where the individual was trapped. With the aid of spotting scopes, researchers can identify individual birds from up to 150 yards away by cueing in on the numbers, letters, and colors on the bands. In this way information can be taken without recapturing the birds.

Varland and his research crew have banded more than one hundred Peregrines since the study began. Seventy-nine percent of those birds were Peale's subspecies, 15 percent could not be identified to subspecies, and the remaining 6 percent of the birds were split evenly between the Continental and Tundra subspecies.

The researchers have been doing this for so long that they often recognize individuals even without the help of scopes or leg bands. One favorite Peregrine Falcon earned the nickname Casino Girl because of her fondness for hanging out near a casino on the beach. At the beginning of each season, the crew is excited to see old acquaintances and catch new participants in this fascinating study.

The color bands indicate trapping location and subspecies for this Peregrine on the Washington coast, studied by the Coastal Raptor Monitoring project. —DAN VARLAND

where the individual animal has been feeding. Certain tissues such as hair, nails, and feathers are inert, or no longer metabolically active after initial growth. By clipping a few feathers from trapped migrants and identifying the stable isotopes present, the geographic origin can be determined. Where the feather was grown indicates natal (spring) or molt (summer) location, so details of each migrant's place of origin are now known. With shrinking costs and greater availability, stable isotope analysis is a safe and effective way to test huge numbers of migrating raptors.

Migration research typically occurs in certain geographic locations that focus raptor movements. Migration bottlenecks are areas of the landscape that experience regular bird concentrations and massing. They are usually associated with a geographical barrier, such as a large body of water or mountain range that raptors are reluctant or unable to cross, or a natural leading line such as a coastline or ridgeline that concentrates movement. Great numbers of birds converge on an isthmus or peninsula. These bottlenecks can be predictable and reliable places to look for raptors for fun or research. Whereas nocturnal songbird migration is observed indirectly using silhouettes of birds migrating in front of a full moon, listening for calls, or using radar, raptor migration counts are done through the direct observation and counting of each bird. Depending on observer experience, the quality of data varies considerably.

One of the most amazing sights on earth is the "super-flocks" of raptors that migrate through Veracruz, Mexico, each fall. The largest and most famous raptor migration on earth, it is called *Río de Rapaces* (River of Raptors). Every year, 2 to 5 million raptors migrate south through this area during a two- to three-month period in the autumn. A mountain range that reaches the Gulf of Mexico funnels the birds through a small area pinched between land and sea. Observations are made at several sites, including the roof of Hotel Bienvenido in the city of Cardel. On a peak day in October, tens of thousands of hawks and vultures may rise in vortices, forming massed, multispecies flocks of soaring raptors. At the top of the thermal, all raptors stream south, forming an aerial river with birds stretching from horizon to horizon. A half million raptors passed over the hotel and count site in an eight-hour period on September 30, 1992, a legendary day in raptor counting. Of the 3.5 million raptors counted in 2006, 3,202 were American Kestrels, 650 were Peregrines, and 131 were Merlins. The telltale flapping flight of a falcon will stand out as it passes by, often at the edges of the main flock. Ironically, the peak migration day in 2006 coincided with the North American Ornithological Conference. The experts were indoors at the raptor migration symposium (some of them, anyway) while their study species streamed overhead.

Important raptor migration corridors are scattered from coast to coast in North America; there are over a thousand count sites in all, with more being discovered every year. The Golden Gate Raptor Observatory (GGRO)

A Peregrine flies near the Bay Bridge, San Francisco, California. —GLEN NEVILL

near San Francisco counted 34,000 raptors in southward migration in 2006, a record high in their more than twenty-year history. Counts included 230 each for Merlins and Peregrines. They also set two new falcon records in 2006, banding 90 American Kestrels and 57 Merlins. They have seen boom and bust years at GGRO, as factors such as weather, predation, and food availability at breeding can all have an effect on total numbers each season.

HawkWatch International (HWI), based in Salt Lake City, Utah, was founded in the late 1970s and monitors raptor migration at ten sites in eight western states. Their primary hawk count site is located in the Goshute Mountains of Nevada, but they also conduct research at Corpus Christi, Texas, and Veracruz, Mexico. HWI is also very involved in raptor education programs.

Hawk Ridge Bird Observatory in Duluth, Minnesota, is located on the western edge of Lake Superior. Raptors reluctant to cross the large body of water follow the lakeshore toward Duluth on their flight south from Canada and Alaska. Counts began in 1951, and the nature reserve located here was created in 1972 partly because of the known raptor migration. Observers counted 111 Peregrines passing through in 1999 and have banded 68 since 1972. Also since 1972, 1,531 American Kestrels and 827 Merlins have been trapped and banded.

Holiday Beach Migration Observatory, on the north end of Lake Erie in Ontario, in 2006 reported a 151 percent increase of Peregrine numbers from the five-year average. That year they counted 114 Peregrines, up from just 15 in 2004.

The Hawk Mountain Sanctuary in Pennsylvania, established in 1934, was the world's first privately owned refuge devoted to birds of prey. Its original use was as a gathering place for gunners shooting migrating raptors. Annual counts begun in the 1930s documented the long-term decline in eastern Peregrine Falcons during the DDT era from the 1940s to the 1990s. In 2006 Hawk Mountain had their highest raptor count in twenty years, with over 25,000 hawks, eagles, and falcons passing by in migration. Because of their dedication and long-term commitment, counters at the Hawk Mountain Sanctuary have the longest running tally of species and numbers of migrant raptors in North America. In addition, the sanctuary is an extremely popular location for visitors and hosts over sixty thousand avid birders each year.

The hawkwatching term *kettle*, familiar to all hawkwatchers, may come from a feature at Hawk Mountain Sanctuary. A nearby depression on the landscape was called *der Kessel* by local German settlers. This type of kettle forms when a block of ice buried by glacial sediment melts, and the sediment above it collapses, leaving a shallow hole or pond. But for hawkwatchers, *kettle* also refers to a flock of raptors circling together in a thermal. This specific location on Kittatinny Ridge has long been a concentration point for kettling buteos (particularly Broad-winged Hawks). An alternative theory on the source of the name is that the swirling raptors look like a boiling kettle.

Cape May Bird Observatory in New Jersey is one of the most famous raptor migration sites in North America. On one spectacular day in 1977, 21,800 raptors passed overhead. Located on a peninsula along the Atlantic shoreline, it consistently produces the highest number of banded raptors in the world. Migrant raptors funnel over this landform in huge numbers when the weather conditions are just right. When north and northwest winds follow a cold front, migrant raptors are pushed right to the coastline. On a single day in 1999, hawkwatchers counted 5,038 American Kestrels and 867 Merlins. During migration, it is not unusual to see three species of falcons (American Kestrels, Merlins, and Peregrines) "in the same field of view at Cape May," reported Jerry Liguori.

The Hawk Migration Association of North America (HMANA) collects data from nearly two hundred count sites in the United States, Canada, and Mexico each year. They publish a semiannual journal listing hawk migration data and discussing current raptor issues. In cooperation with Hawk Mountain Sanctuary and HawkWatch International, they compile the Raptor Population Index (RPI) to promote conservation, education, and awareness of migrating birds of prey. The RPI is designed to track raptor populations on a local, regional, and national level.

Hawk Mountain Sanctuary in Pennsylvania, established in 1934, is the world's first privately owned refuge for raptors. Keith Bildstein explains how tens of thousands of raptors per year fly past this spot, which was formerly used as a shooting gallery. —KATE DAVIS

Data collected across the continent suggest some alarming trends in raptor numbers. In 2006 eastern continental American Kestrel numbers dropped 47.8 percent from recent averages. Ernesto Ruelas Inzunza of HMANA suggested that this could be a result of environmental contaminants, forest succession limiting habitat types, increased predation from Cooper's Hawks, or West Nile virus. The RPI will let scientists know if this trend continues.

HMANA and other professional organizations and scientists are also exploring the negative effects of turbines at wind farms on birds and bats, a threat that some raptor ecologists envision may be as devastating as DDT. They feel that preconstruction evaluations of the dangers posed to migrants are inadequate and inaccurate, and that fatal collisions could kill 1.8 million birds per year by the year 2030. A large percentage of these collisions may involve raptors. Other worries on the horizon are migratory changes of raptors and prey species due to climate change. With the detailed databases provided by hawkwatchers across the continent we can understand these dangers more readily and respond to them.

In medieval times, the white phase variant of the Gyrfalcon was reserved for the king with the most clout. —ROB PALMER

—5—

Falcons and Humankind

Humans have been fascinated with falcons since prehistory; falcon images adorn petroglyphs, ancient coins, statues, paintings, and the Egyptian pyramids. People have perceived falcons as somehow more noble than other birds. In her book *Falcon*, Helen Macdonald writes that falcons are associated with "refinement, strength, independence, superiority, the power of life and death over others."

Falcons have been important totems for many cultures, bringing the qualities of these birds to humans: speed, power, and fortunate hunting. Presented as diplomatic gifts to curry favor or patch up disputes, falcons are to this day a form of living currency. For example, in the 1970s the U.S. State Department used Gyrfalcons and Continental Peregrine Falcons as gifts to kings and princes during negotiations with oil-rich countries in the Middle East.

FALCON GODS

Eagles, hawks, and condors were probably among the first raptors to be depicted in folklore and religion, starting with pictographs in early cave paintings. Falcons also had important roles throughout recorded history and were significant in ancient Egyptian religion and mythology. The Egyptian god Horus, meaning "Lofty One," was probably one of the best-known falcons in historic tradition. Horus, a creator god, flew from heaven at the beginning of time. He appeared in statues as a falcon or a man with a falcon head and in hieroglyphs associated with kings, his earthly personification. Kestrels, Lanners, and many other species of falcons were mummified through time, and hundreds of thousands were given as offerings to the Egyptian gods. One temple to Isis, the mother of Horus, contained one hundred thousand falcons dipped in tar, preserved, and sealed in coffins or stacked in rows of jars. Trade in falcons for this purpose was widespread, and wild falcons were trapped, which must have affected bird populations at the time.

In North America, the story of the Thunderbird is widespread among indigenous peoples. Thunderbird was a huge, all-powerful raptor that personified thunder, lightning, and even rainfall. He reached across the continent and took many forms. For the Northwest Coastal tribes, he created the world itself. The Plains tribes believed that thunderstorms were a competition between the raptor and a giant rattlesnake. To Southeastern indigenous people, Thunderbird carried their prayers for rain to the creator. Although often depicted as an eagle or vulture, the Thunderbird could well be a falcon. Masks found in the Linear Mounds Archaeological site of Manitoba, Canada, depict Peregrines, with the dark malar stripe painted below the eyehole. When shown these relics, Native elders from the southeastern United States recognize them as the Thunderbird. The giant raptor was also important to Central American tribes who believed he was the cause of storms.

Falcons were revered across North America and often seen as messengers between humans and the spirit world. The shaman in many North American Native cultures became a falcon while in an ecstatic trance state in order to travel between different worlds. He or she could visit heaven or the underworld, and guide souls to their final resting place. For the Plains peoples, only a falcon knew the place of the hole in the sky. The shaman's or elder's questions could be answered by the deities when the falcon flew to the heavens and back.

Powers granted by falcons protected humans, and a Crow Indian shield from Montana depicted a Prairie Falcon and feathers. The falcon was the owner's protecting genius and the feathers were prayers.

MODERN CULTURE

Falcons, used as modern-day totems, maintain their role as a fixture in contemporary popular culture. The name *falcon* lends positive values and clout. Obvious examples are the Ford Falcon automobile of the 1960s, Atlanta Falcons football team, and mascots for thousands of school sports teams. The U.S. Air Force boasts that, reminiscent of its namesake, the F-16 Fighting Falcon can pull 9 Gs, deftly engage in air-to-air combat, and locate targets in every type of weather. A vast array of companies use the name, from FalconGuides outdoor recreation books and Falcon Communications to Falcon Waterfree Urinals. Product lines range from fishing rods and commercial furniture to a hypersonic cruise vehicle. In film, they have been immortalized by *The Maltese Falcon* by John Huston and the *Millennium Falcon* of *Star Wars* fame. Falcon species are similarly honored by Kestrel Wines, British Merlin attack helicopters, the 210-mile Prairie Falcon Parkway Express in Colorado, Peregrine Pharmaceuticals, Gyrfalcon.net, and Aplomado.com.

FALCONRY IN HISTORY

One of the closest relationships humans have had with raptors has been through falconry, the sport of hunting wild game with a trained raptor. Falcons have generally been preferred over other raptors since the sport began about four thousand years ago, perhaps earlier.

The origins of falconry are unknown. Unlike preserved artifacts of prehistory such as flint or stone spears, arrowheads, and tools, falconry paraphernalia is made of cord, leather, and sinew, all of which readily decompose. French falconer M. A. Brosset noticed scavenging raptors following him while he was hunting; these birds later converged on the gut pile of animals he killed. Brosset suggested something similar may have occurred for primitive humans, who often set traps to catch animals. Popular thinking is that early humans who were trapping birds for food figured out that raptors capture animals and could be trained to do so for human benefit.

While the early history of the sport is not clear, it may have started in China, the Mongolian steppes, the Arabian Peninsula, Persia (Iran), or India around 2000 BC. What most likely started as way of securing food for survival underwent a gradual transformation and became a sport. The Great Khans, rulers in Central Asia, kept falcons to catch food around 1000 BC; they also used falcons for sport on military campaigns. Marco Polo wrote in awed terms of Kublai Khan, saying he was accompanied on his expeditions by more than ten thousand falconers and hundreds of Gyrfalcons, Peregrines, and Sakers.

A Peregrine Falcon trains after a summer spent eating a rich diet of quail, molting, and growing new feathers, all in preparation for the seven-month hunting season. —KATE DAVIS

Telemetry is a relatively new innovation in the four-thousand-year-old sport of falconry. This Merlin has a lightweight neck mount that allows the bird to be tracked using a receiver.
—ROB PALMER

In the Middle East, falconry is culturally integrated into modern society. Fifty percent of the world's falconers live in the Middle East. The Holy Koran describes falconry as an accepted form of hunting to teach bravery, stamina, perseverance, and self-reliance. In China falconry was inseparable from politics and power, and the techniques of the ancient Chinese continue to be practiced in modern times.

Falconry earned a high level of reverence, popularity, and protection in Europe during the Middle Ages (from around 500–1600 AD). At different times the sport was either reserved for the noble classes or part of everyday life for all social strata. However, the great respect for raptors came to an end in Europe in the early 1600s. The feudal system dissolved, and land was cleared for agriculture. Effective firearms were perfected, and shooting became the preferred sport. Falconers and wild raptors were both in direct competition with the gun hunters, taking game that was reserved for the landowner, not birds of prey.

MODERN FALCONRY IN NORTH AMERICA

Present-day falconry has been described as a specialized form of birdwatching, with humans as spectators while the falcons go about their instinctive behaviors of flight, pursuit, and killing of prey. Falconry is a sport of positive

This hybrid falcon, called a Gyr/Peregrine by falconers, was produced by artificial insemination between a male black Gyrfalcon and a female Peale's Peregrine. —KATE DAVIS

reinforcement. The basic premise is to reward the captive raptor for a desired behavior—in this case the reward is food. So the answer to the eternal question, Why do they come back? is simple. They are hungry enough to want to do so. But there is a fine line between keeping a bird "sharp set," or at a great flying weight, and being so famished that it will be weakened. The reverse is also a problem. If the bird is overweight it will have no incentive to hunt and may go perch in a tree for a day or two.

Falconry had a slow start in North America, and very few people practiced the sport until the early 1900s. One of the catalysts may have been the December 1920 issue of *National Geographic*. The magazine featured a forty-page story by Louis Agassiz Fuertes called "Falconry, the Sport of Kings," richly illustrated with his signature paintings. Another catalyst was R. L. Meredith's book *American Falconry in the Twentieth Century*, completed in the 1930s. These two publications served as introductions for many people, including

A trained Aplomado Falcon flies over the prairie of Colorado. This particular bird became adept at catching doves but was tragically killed by a Red-tailed Hawk. —ROB PALMER

young naturalists John and Frank Craighead, who were so taken that they began training raptors on their own. In the July 1937 issue of *National Geographic*, in an article called "Adventures with Birds of Prey," the twin brothers described the experiences they had begun six years earlier as teenagers in the wilds of the Potomac River near their home in Washington, D.C. They followed up with their classic book *Hawks in the Hand* in 1939. The Craigheads spent nine months hunting in India and penned another *National Geographic* article in 1941, "Life with an Indian Prince," and produced a documentary film by the same name.

The U.S. Fish and Wildlife Service created falconry regulations in 1964, permitting wild falcons to be taken and trained to hunt game birds in established seasons. Additional federal regulations in 1976 were the result of more public input. From just two public notices requesting opinions, sixteen thousand comments from organizations and individuals were received, the largest number of public comments ever submitted on a U.S. Fish and Wildlife Service proposal at the time. New regulations established three classes of permits, identified species allowed for use, and set the standards of falconer experience, in addition to mandatory housing and banding of falconry birds. The sport was still not allowed in some states at the time, but interest was growing.

Apprentice falconers may keep an American Kestrel (pictured here) or a Red-tailed Hawk in most of the United States. After a two-year learning period, a general falconer may keep up to two raptors of other species (excluding eagles). —KATE DAVIS

It is believed that raptor populations are not affected by the taking of wild birds for the sport. In 2006 the U.S. Fish and Wildlife Service conducted a study to determine a reasonable harvest rate, or take, for various species of wild raptors. They recommended that a maximum of 5 percent of juvenile raptors produced in a year be taken for species for which demographic data are available (Peregrines, Northern Goshawks, and Golden Eagles). Lesser-studied species should have a 1 percent harvest rate until data can confirm that a larger percentage is possible.

This study also revealed that the actual numbers of birds taken from the wild for the sport are well below the recommended maximum of 5 percent or 1 percent. In 2007, some western states allowed the taking of eyas (fledgling) Peregrines by falconers. The U.S. Fish and Wildlife Service will make a decision in 2008 on allowing the taking of passage Peregrines (first-year birds passing in migration), which was ended when the species was first listed as endangered. Also in 2008, the U.S. Fish and Wildlife Service is expected to issue updated regulations governing falconry. These regulations will "account

for the low impact of the sport on wild populations, and will recognize recent changes in the practice of the sport."

Gyrfalcons and Peregrines need wide open spaces for hunting, which limits the sport in much of the continent. Gyrfalcons—birds of the Arctic—are intolerant of excessive heat and humidity, and when kept in warmer climates are prone to contracting debilitating diseases. Prairie Falcons also need open space, but they provide the added complication of having the reputation of being stubborn and difficult to train. Merlins are used to hunt starlings in cattle pastures, and in the United States, American Kestrels may be used to hunt House Sparrows out of the window of a car. Aplomado Falcons are now available from breeders and have proven to be great hunters of quail and doves. No matter what the tactic, the sport is time-consuming. It is beyond a hobby; for the devoted falconer it is an art and a lifestyle.

There are approximately five thousand licensed falconers in the United States today, and it is no longer a sport for kings alone. The biggest demographic increase in the sport has been for women, who are taking their place in falconry. The sport has endured and will certainly have devoted participants as long as falcons and quarry exist.

Some captive falcons are used for work and not just pleasure, from nuisance bird mitigation to flight displays. Trained falcons have recently been found to be very effective at patrolling airport runways to reduce collisions between aircraft and other birds. Collisions are costly and can be deadly, and businesses dedicated to bird abatement have been formed. The United States Air Force Academy has a falconry program available to cadets, who train birds to fly during halftime events of football games in front of tens of thousands of fans. Falconry birds are also increasingly popular in flight demonstrations at zoos and wild animal parks, increasing public awareness of raptors and the importance of habitat preservation. Jemima Parry-Jones points out that the problem with such demonstrations is that "done well, the birds should fly well and the whole thing look very easy—unfortunately it looks too easy for those who fancy trying it themselves."

Falcons on blocks in the weathering yard at a North American Falconers Association meet in Liberal, Kansas. Once a year members gather for a week of flying and exchanging information, stories, and insight. —ROB PALMER

A captive-bred Aplomado Falcon in flight. This is the South American subspecies, with the characteristic buff-colored underparts. —ROB PALMER

6

Falcon Conservation

Despite the reverence and respect that many people have for falcons, humans have contributed greatly to their plight. Their population plunges were seen as alarm calls to action in an environmental crisis. They are top predators at the pinnacle of the food chain, and their role as barometers of ecosystem health shouldn't be overlooked. Falcons became charismatic macrofauna and front-page news during the crisis caused by the pesticide DDT. Their declines, along with the extinction of the eastern Peregrine race, served to warn humans of the danger of increasingly relying on "better living through chemistry." The future of falcon populations is still not certain to this day.

Based on the population trajectory in the 1960s, a world without Peregrine Falcons could have been a reality, and some Peregrine specialists wrote obituaries of the species' impending extinction. While this scenario didn't happen, many feel that it came disastrously close, and without human intervention Peregrines may well have disappeared for good. Equally hard to imagine is a wide-open field without an American Kestrel hovering in the wind, but American Kestrel populations have sharply declined in much of eastern North America in the late 1990s. The fast-coursing flight of the Prairie Falcon is also becoming less common in places where urban sprawl has replaced open fields. To ensure the chance of glimpsing a Gyrfalcon standing on a snowy outcrop, we must wait and see if they benefit from being assigned the highest protection status through CITES (Convention on International Trade in Endangered Species), a global agreement designed to safeguard more than thirty thousand species of plants and animals. The human-caused hazards facing raptors today are diverse and affect other species too. As biological indicators of environmental contaminants, falcons can give us insight into the health of humankind, as well.

The most severe problem currently facing raptors worldwide is the degradation and loss of habitat. Human populations alter the environment through agriculture and development, and what habitat is left is isolated from other tracts. All native species suffer as a result. Invasive exotic species also adversely affect ecosystem health and plant and animal well-being.

A female or juvenile Richardson's Merlin perches on a fence. Note the light supercilliary line, faint malar stripe, and darkish eye line.
—ROB PALMER

Extirpation, or local extinction, means that a species is no longer present in an area it once inhabited, but still remains elsewhere. For example, the Peregrine was wiped out east of the Mississippi River and nearly extirpated from the rest of the North American continent. Reproductive success declined because of the effects of the pesticide DDT. With poor reproduction, the population of floaters—unattached adults of breeding age that step in when one mate in a falcon pair dies—became nonexistent. The Northern Aplomado Falcon was extirpated from the United States because of alterations to its habitat. Despite large population declines, neither of these birds became extinct, and populations on other continents fared better.

RAPTORS AS ENEMIES

As recently as the mid-1900s, falcons and other raptors were considered by farmers and hunters as enemies or targets, sometimes with a substantial reward for their killing. Pennsylvania even had the Scalp Act, which targeted all birds of prey. In a survey at the time, 90 percent of the state residents

Peregrine Falcons, like all birds of prey, are now protected by law.
—ROB PALMER

believed it was a good plan. During the heyday of this destruction, from about 1860 to as late as 1960, hundreds of thousands of raptors across the continent were trapped, shot, and poisoned, persecuted as wanton killers of wild game birds and captive fowl. Predators like bobcats, foxes, coyotes, wolves, and bears were similarly exterminated.

It is doubtful that the nineteenth- and twentieth-century bounty hunters could tell the difference between a good and bad hawk. Consequently, all raptors suffered indiscriminate shooting and killing. In an effort to educate the public in Montana, one 1935 flyer described which birds should and should not be protected, depending on their diet of fowl or "injurious rodents." Some migration routes were popular shooting locations, such as Cape May Point, New Jersey, and Hawk Mountain, Pennsylvania. Photographs depict hawk carcasses piled up to 6 feet high. Richard Pough writes of picking up 218 raptors killed in one hour at Hawk Mountain in 1932.

Another group killing raptors in the misguided spirit of guarding their sport were and are the pigeon racers and pigeon fanciers. While valuable

# RAPTOR RESEARCH FOUNDATION

In 1966, thirteen raptor biologists and falconers gathered in Madison, Wisconsin, to discuss the fate of the Peregrine Falcon in what turned out to be the first meeting of the Raptor Research Foundation. Alarmed by the Peregrine's declining populations in North America, the organizers hoped to help the birds avoid extinction by starting a captive breeding program. Although the men and women were primarily concerned about the decline of the Peregrine Falcon, they also wanted to get people interested in other birds of prey by making scientific information about these fascinating creatures more accessible and easier to understand.

Like the Peregrine Falcon's rebounding population, the Raptor Research Foundation has grown by leaps and bounds over the years. It distributes information about birds of prey and works to encourage the respect for raptors worldwide. The foundation has published several books of collected papers, including *Raptors in Human Landscapes* and *Raptor Research and Management Techniques.* Their original newsletter, *Raptor Research News*, is now called the *Journal of Raptor Research*, and publishes peer-reviewed papers about scientific research being conducted on birds of prey. The foundation now has more than one thousand members from some fifty countries.

Two recently fledged sibling Peregrines hone their flying skills with playful encounters.
—NICK DUNLOP

Dead hawks lined up in rows at Hawk Mountain. —ARCHIVAL PHOTO FROM HAWK MOUNTAIN SANCTUARY, COURTESY OF KEITH BILDSTEIN

homing and racing pigeons have long been killed by Peregrines, quite often falcons were scapegoats for other factors that affected the pigeons, such as inclement weather. In England during World War II, the Destruction of Peregrine Falcons Order was issued in 1940 to protect carrier pigeons. Military messages were attached to the legs of homing pigeons on battlefields in mainland Europe, and the birds flew back to bases in Great Britain to deliver vital information. For the good of the nation, the pigeons' predators were to be exterminated. More than six hundred Peregrines were shot during the war, and countless young and eggs were destroyed.

OTHER LOSSES

In the mid-1800s, egg collecting became popular as a hobby and for professional study. Egg collectors, or professional oologists, found falcon eggs—with their striking spots and mottling—particularly beautiful. Because they were relatively uncommon, eggs from cliff nesters were highly valued. They were also difficult to acquire with the rudimentary climbing gear of the time (sisal rope and a lot of nerve). Falcons were not protected by law, so collectors could take eggs from the same nests and regions year after year. Generally all the eggs in a clutch were taken because they were prized as a full set. In 1883, one popular Peregrine eyrie had more than thirty egg collectors climb the cliff to it in one day in attempts to secure its single clutch of eggs. By the 1940s this pastime was falling from favor. In an ironic twist, egg sets collected before 1946 were critical in helping scientists determine that a major cause of the Peregrine population crash was thinning—and ultimate breaking—of the eggs caused by the pesticide DDT. This information has helped protect Peregrines to the present day.

By the early 1900s, commercial trade in wild birds of all species was having severe detrimental effects on population numbers. Plumed birds such as egrets and herons were being wiped out so their feathers and wings could be used as decorations for women's hats. Passenger pigeons, once numbering in the billions, became extinct due to sport shooting. Because of these tragic losses, conservationists of that era forced Congress to enact the Migratory Bird Protection Act in 1918, an agreement between Canada and the United States designed to protect nongame birds. The Bald Eagle Protection Act was created in 1940 and amended in 1962 to include the Golden Eagle. Attitudes

This female Peregrine and her newly hatched chick were photographed in 1971 at the nest in Bathurst Inlet, Northwest Territories, Canada.
—RON AUSTING

about raptors slowly began to change. Spurred on by scientists such as Aldo Leopold and John and Frank Craighead, ecology became a credible science, and conservation of keystone predators became a topic of concern.

PESTICIDES

By far the biggest impact of the twentieth century on some raptors has been through synthetic chemicals. Raptors are often found at the upper levels of food chains, and therefore are often most severely affected. Fish eaters, or piscivores (Bald Eagles and Ospreys), and bird eaters, or avivores (Peregrine Falcons), suffered severe population declines in North America from the mid-1940s until just recently.

The compound DDT (dichloro-diphenyl-trichloroethane) was first synthesized in the 1890s but was used sparingly until World War II. Wide-ranging uses during the war included human delousing and clearing swamps of malaria-carrying mosquitoes to make areas safer for occupying allied forces. Huge quantities of the chemical were manufactured for the war, and stockpiles that became surplus after the war were released for commercial use in 1946. DDT is easily manufactured, inexpensive, and very effective. A broad-spectrum pesticide, it kills a variety of insects. Chemist Paul Muller earned a Nobel Prize in 1948 for developing this "wonder chemical." Other pesticides that have affected raptors worldwide include aldrin, dieldrin, endrin, and heptachlor. All of these compounds are stable and persist for long periods in the environment. In addition, they are lipophilic, or fat loving, and are stored in the fatty tissues of animals which allows these compounds to bioaccumulate in the bodies of predators.

DDT is metabolized into the compound DDE (dichloro-diphenyl-dicholoroethylene), which is also retained in the body's fatty, or adipose, tissues. DDE is released into the bloodstream when the adipose tissue is metabolized for energy. This release occurs at times of physiological stress, such as reproduction and egg formation. Birds that eat fish or birds are often most affected, as their prey have long, complex food cycles. For example, tiny invertebrates that have accumulated DDE are ingested by insects, which are in turn eaten by fish, which are then eaten by larger fish, and so on, with the DDE bioaccumulating at higher levels in each organism up the food web. By the time a Brown Pelican, Bald Eagle, or Osprey feeds on the larger fish, the DDE levels are high enough to negatively affect reproduction and, in some cases, physiology and behavior.

DDE prevents two important enzymes from allowing calcium and carbonate to form the outermost eggshell layer when the egg is being made in the female bird's uterus. The higher the concentrations of DDE is in the female's body, the thinner the eggshell is. Extremely thin eggshells reduce the strength

A Peregrine Falcon with a Killdeer for food. As bird eaters, Peregrines are high on the food chain and at risk for accumulating toxins in their bodies.
—NICK DUNLOP

of the egg, which the adult may break during incubation. The porosity of the shell is also affected, so embryo respiration and gas exchange are disrupted, resulting in the death of the developing chick. Membrane slippage within the egg can also cause death.

High DDE levels also change adult endocrine levels and induce other behaviors detrimental to reproduction. Parent birds have been seen to nest very late, or not all, and eat their eggs in the eyrie. Populations of raptors dropped precipitously in the 1940s and 1950s. Few young birds were being produced to replace old birds as they died, with recruitment in much of the continent at zero.

PEREGRINE EXTIRPATION AND REINTRODUCTION

Pigeon fanciers in Great Britain started efforts to investigate pesticides, in a roundabout way. In an effort to protect their racing and tumbler pigeons, they asked the government to remove the Peregrine from the protected list so that Peregrines could be legally killed. Derek Ratcliffe of the British Nature Conservancy was given the task of assessing falcon numbers in 1960. As head of the Peregrine Enquiry for the British Trust for Ornithology, he conducted a two-year survey across Great Britain and Northern Ireland. Ratcliffe knew

Peregrine Falcons had recovered modestly from eradication efforts during World War II. However, Peregrine numbers had been dropping in recent years for unknown reasons. By then, populations around most of the United Kingdom were 68 percent less than previous known numbers. Ratcliffe and others watched known Peregrine nest sites suffer widespread reproductive failure. Nests had broken eggs, some female Peregrine Falcons were not laying eggs at all, and far fewer young were produced than in previous decades. These failures coincided with the spraying of organochlorine pesticides like DDT. Because of this study, Derek Ratcliffe is often credited with first noting that eggshell thinning was responsible for reproductive failure,

Inspired by these findings, Joseph J. Hickey noted eggshell thinning in twenty-two species of birds in the United States, including raptors and birds who feed on fish. By the 1960s, Peregrines were extirpated east of the Mississippi River. They existed at just a fraction of their numbers in the west and were completely gone from Montana, Wyoming, Oregon, and Washington, as well as Alberta, Canada. There were just fifteen known pairs in all of Colorado and New Mexico, four pairs in Utah and Arizona, and two pairs in California. (The word *known* is used as some nests were probably missed in the surveys.)

A Peregrine Falcon circles.
—NICK DUNLOP

In 1962, Rachel Carson's book *Silent Spring* called for companies and citizens to cease pesticide use. She presented to the lay audience the detrimental effects of pesticides and disinformation spread by the chemical industry. Her efforts inspired concern and calls for change from ordinary citizens.

Biologists and land managers concerned with the fate of the Peregrine Falcon in North America gathered for what would be called the 1965 Madison Conference, organized by Joseph Hickey. Scientific evidence suggesting pesticides as a cause of the population decline was presented, and efforts to

PEREGRINES RETURN TO MONTANA

By 1980 the Peregrine Falcon was gone from Montana. Efforts were made to reestablish the bird at an ideal location, the remote Red Rock Lakes National Wildlife Refuge in the Centennial Valley near Yellowstone National Park. Here, dramatic mountains rising 9,000 feet from the valley floor surround vast wetlands. Starting in 1981, 45 falcons were released at three hack sites in Red Rocks.

Terry McEneaney was the staff ornithologist at Yellowstone for more than thirty years and is one of the finest birders in the region. He recounts the day in June 1984 when he and his wife were viewing wildlife in the Centennial Valley at sundown. Four trumpeter swans were crossing the Centennial Mountains when suddenly the group plunged from the sky. Their huge white shapes could be seen crashing into the tree canopy below. McEneaney told his wife, "There are only two things that could panic a bird like that, and since we didn't see a Golden Eagle, it had to be a Peregrine." The next day he returned to the area and found the first nesting Peregrines known in the state since their extirpation. This territorial attack was on a bird more than ten times their size! It turns out that these Peregrines were former hack site birds, and Peregrines have produced young there every year since. McEneaney has located 25 eyries in the Yellowstone ecosystem, which attests to the Peregrine's phenomenal recovery as well as his birding skills. He has observed Peregrines in the area on several occasions feeding on fish, an anomaly for a bird-catching specialist.

2007 Peregrine statistics are encouraging, with 68 active Peregrine nests fledging 108 birds throughout the state of Montana.

save Peregrine subspecies from extinction in North America were launched. Almost all populations of Peregrines were declining worldwide, and some researchers feared their complete extinction. The goal was to breed falcons in captivity for release back to the wild if the environment recovered. A 1969 study of captive American Kestrels by Jeffrey Lincer of Cornell University further showed pesticide use resulted in reproductive failure. He also found that polychlorinated biphenyls (PCBs) affected their metabolism. PCBs were added to DDT and dieldrin and used widely in the manufacture of plastics and in electrical transformers.

In 1970, two subspecies of Peregrines in the United States were placed on the federal list of endangered species. The Tundra subspecies (*F. peregrinus tundrius*) of the far north and the Continental subspecies (*F. p. anatum*) were considered endangered. The Pacific Northwest Coastal Peale's subspecies (*F. p. pealei*) was thought to be less affected and was not listed. The other big event of 1970 was the formation of the Peregrine Fund by Tom Cade of Cornell University. Five years later the Santa Cruz Predatory Bird Research Group was formed. The mission of these organizations was to reestablish the Peregrine Falcon in the wild before it was too late. However, the greatest benefit to the Peregrine Falcon and numerous other bird species was the banning of DDT use in Canada in 1969 and in the United States in 1972.

With the help of state and federal government agencies, private corporations, and individuals, a continent-wide breeding program was created for Peregrines. This was no small task as few people had bred falcons in captivity before. Further, because of federal listing in 1970, it was not possible to obtain federal permits to take wild stock because of extremely low wild populations. It was decided that Continental Peregrines (*F. p. anatum*) already in breeding facilities would be used for captive breeding. Other subspecies were also used to produce Peregrines for reintroduction in the eastern United States. At the 1974 conference on Peregrine Falcon recovery, the group recommended to the U.S. Fish and Wildlife Service that "the eastern recovery program be based on introduction of the most promising, ecologically pre-adapted stock available regardless of geographic origin." In addition to the three North American subspecies, the following were used in the eastern United States to produce what was perceived as a new subspecies for a new time: *F. peregrinus peregrinus* from Scotland, *F. p. brookei* from Spain, *F. p. cassini* from Chile, and *F. p. macropus* from Australia.

Richard Fyfe led the Canadian Peregrine Falcon recovery program, which opted to use only the North American Continental subspecies, *F. p. anatum*. A small number of birds of this subspecies were taken from the wild for breeding. Efforts for reintroduction in the western United States also used the Continental subspecies.

Early in the recovery program, some captive-bred Peregrines were fostered into wild Peregrine nests; others were cross-fostered into wild Prairie Falcon nests. The most widely used method was through hacking. The intention of hacking was to take thirty-seven- to thirty-eight-day-old Peregrine chicks from breeders and place them in plywood containers called hack boxes, a technique originally borrowed from falconers. Hack boxes were placed on natural cliffs or on specially constructed towers, giving the young birds a

 THE PEREGRINE FUND

The threat of losing the Peregrine in North America became a rallying cry for falcon aficionados throughout the world. Perhaps the most ambitious organization was formed in 1970. Under the leadership of Tom Cade, professor of ornithology at Cornell University, the nonprofit Peregrine Fund began, initially for the purpose of breeding peregrines for reintroduction. Their early facilities were in a pole barn at Cornell; they eventually moved to a former research station outside Fort Collins, Colorado. Falconers and collectors donated birds to the breeding efforts, which until then had been mostly unsuccessful. The researchers used techniques pioneered by falconers: artificial insemination and double clutching, or removing eggs so the female will produce a second batch.

The Peregrine Fund flourished with private, corporate, and governmental support. Reintroduction began in 1974, another technique borrowed from falconers. The largest conservation effort of any animal at any time celebrated victory when the Peregrine was delisted as an endangered species in 1999. The gala event was held at the World Center for Birds of Prey in Boise, Idaho, the Fund's state-of-the-art breeding, research and educational facility that opened in 1984. This is also the location of the Archives of American Falconry.

Today the World Center houses about 200 falcons and California Condors for breeding. Their goal is to "propagate the required

full view of their future surrounding hunting grounds. Hack site attendants fed the chicks whole quail dropped in through a feeding tube so the birds wouldn't associate food with humans. At forty-five days of age, the falcons were released by opening up the front of the hack box. The youngsters usually remained around their artificial nest for four or five weeks after fledging. Attendants continued feeding the birds until they became skilled at hunting on their own and dispersed.

number of the best possible physically, behaviorally, and genetically constituted raptors for release to the wild." The P-Fund's efforts go way beyond this country, and extend from Gyrfalcon work in the Arctic to Asian vultures, Harpy Eagles in Panama, and education in Africa and the West Indies. The group has been instrumental in restoring the critically endangered Mauritius Kestrel and is seeing progress with the Aplomado Falcon. The Peregrine Fund boasts that 95% of their revenue goes directly to programs, and that they are "working to conserve birds of prey in nature." There will no doubt be more victories to celebrate in the future.

A Peregrine on the move. —KATE DAVIS

An urban Peregrine investigates the photographer. —ROB PALMER

Peregrines normally breed between two to four years of age, and a large number of hacked birds returned to their former hack sites or found new territories nearby. Curiously, researchers observed many one-year-old birds breeding during the reintroduction program, a year or more younger than expected. Reestablishing Peregrine populations relied on the behavior of nest site fidelity, with birds returning to the area they were raised. More than seven thousand Peregrines were released in North America over thirty years, mostly out of hack boxes. The first successful Peregine breeding in the east in over twenty years occurred in 1980 from hacked chicks. Never has such an all-encompassing project been attempted to restore an animal population.

In 1994 the Tundra Peregrine (*F. p. tundrius*), breeder of the far north, was delisted, or removed, from the U.S. endangered species list. In August of 1999, at a ceremony at the Peregrine Fund's World Center for Birds of Prey in Boise, Idaho, the Continental Peregrine Falcon (*F. P. anatum*) was removed from the U.S. Endangered Species list. Prior to that time, critics argued that delisting was premature, and the falcons should first be downlisted to threatened.

Several researchers believe Peregrines have surpassed their pre-DDT population numbers; this opinion, however, remains controversial. *The Birds of North America* account estimates that eight thousand to ten thousand breeding pairs of all three subspecies were present in North America in 2000, with numbers increasing. Although many historic nest sites have not been reoccupied, others have higher breeding densities than before extirpation. Sites not used in the past—city buildings, power plants, and bridges—are being used by many populations of breeding Peregrines.

The mixture of subspecies that were bred and released in the eastern United States may have resulted in a new subspecies for a post-DDT world. Brian Wheeler designates eastern Peregrines as "Eastern (no subspecies)" in his raptor books. New research suggests that Continental and Tundra Peregrines may be genetically identical. Yet many researchers find them very different both behaviorally and morphologically. Zones of hybridization exist between all three North American subspecies. But many raptor enthusiasts may agree, it is better to see a Peregrine than not, no matter what the genetics.

A fledgling Continental Peregrine at a cliff site in northern California. —NICK DUNLOP

APLOMADO FALCON

The Northern Aplomado Falcon was extirpated from the United States by 1952, gone from grassland habitats on the United States border with Mexico. Its disappearance occurred largely before widespread DDT use but was still caused by humans. The lush native yucca and grassland communities where Aplomado Falcons had historically hunted birds had been altered drastically: converted to agricultural row crops, overgrazed by livestock, and overrun with shrubs like mesquite and creosote. Aplomados were listed as a federally endangered species in February 1986.

Numerous state and federal agencies stepped in with a reintroduction plan. Beginning in 1985, young Aplomados bred by the Santa Cruz Predatory Bird Research Group were hacked out in south Texas. In the 1990s the Peregrine

A falconry Aplomado Falcon successfully captures a Mourning Dove. Where game birds are hunted, falcons and other raptors may ingest lead, which can be lethal. Steel shot is substituted in some areas.
—ROB PALMER

Fund again played a key role in reestablishing a breeding population of an endangered falcon, this time under a new federal program called Safe Harbor. This program afforded some protection to the falcons' habitat, a key component in any successful reintroduction. In a controversial turn of events after the first releases, Aplomados—wild-born as well as hacked birds—in Arizona and New Mexico were federally downgraded to "experimental nonessential" in 2006, which lessened their status of protection under the U.S. Endangered Species Act. Public and private landowners were no longer obliged to protect the birds' habitat outright. Critics have claimed this is a way for the Peregrine Fund to continue to "release, release, release," maintaining a costly breeding program indefinitely. Hack sites have recently been expanded, with new ones established in west Texas, New Mexico, and Mexico.

Some believe the Aplomado Falcon will adjust to the new habitat of the twenty-first century. Nevertheless, recent changes in land use are going to be hard on this falcon. Large-scale oil and gas development is slated for the region, and it is doubtful that the falcons can adapt entirely to these landscape alterations. In Mexico agriculture is reducing native grasslands. A small pocket of naturally breeding Northern Aplomado Falcons exists in the northern state of Chihuahua, most likely a remnant population of those that

A Peregrine glides in the classic falcon flight position, often described as sickle- or anchor-shaped. The second-to-last primary feather is longest and wing tips are pointed. —KATE DAVIS

lived farther north and east. Surrounding grasslands are quickly being bought up and plowed under by corporate farming interests. Studies have shown water supplies for irrigation will run out, yet the land rush is on. Perhaps the high prices given to farmers who grow corn for biofuels will spell disaster for the Aplomado Falcon, along with every other inhabitant of the grassland ecosystem of the southern United States and northern Mexico.

SANTA CRUZ PREDATORY BIRD RESEARCH GROUP

The Santa Cruz Predatory Bird Research Group (SCPBRG) was founded in 1975 as a research, breeding, and recovery center for Peregrine Falcons on the West Coast. It is affiliated with the University of California Institute of Marine Sciences at Santa Cruz. The organization was started by veterinarian Jim Roush, professor Ken Norris, and biologist Brian Walton.

One of the group's first tasks was to determine how many Peregrine Falcons remained in California by locating active nests. They found that the Peregrine's population had plummeted, with just ten birds and two active nests in the state. In 1977, they took two chicks hatched at the Peregrine Fund's Cornell, New York, breeding facility and placed them in the nest of a pair of Peregrines on Morro Rock, a volcanic plug off the coast near San Luis Obispo, California. The tactic worked. Today there are two breeding pairs of falcons on the rock.

SCPBRG established a breeding facility, and eggs with thin shells were taken from remaining nests and placed in an incubator, rather than risk having them crushed by parent birds. Dummy eggs kept the falcons interested and attentive to the nest, and chicks hatched from the first eggs or those from the facility were placed at the eyrie. Foster parenting was successful, as was cross-fostering by having the more common Prairie Falcon raise the young. By 1992 the SCPBRG had released almost 800 Peregrines. The 2006

California Survey identified 271 Peregrine breeding territories. The Bird Group still releases a small number of youngsters each year, in addition to rescuing chicks from dangerous sites such as bridges, where fledgling mortality would most likely be high.

SCPBRG pioneered Aplomado Falcon breeding and reintroduction, producing the first chicks to be hacked out in Texas. A pair from these first 24 birds became the first since their extirpation to successfully reproduce in the wild in the United States. Other current projects for the group include providing information about retrofitting power poles to protect birds and bats from electrocution; protecting Prairie Falcon habitat, as well as the unique Channel Islands ecosystem; and "developing and implementing non-lethal solutions for protecting beach-nesting seabirds from avian predators such as shrikes, hawks, owls, and falcons." Conservation education is a key component, and the original founders would never have dreamed of such a wide-reaching and ambitious agenda.

A webcam set up by the Santa Cruz Predatory Bird Research Group offers glimpses into everyday life of an urban Peregrine family. With the web cam, thousands of raptorphiles can observe the falcons in real time on their computer screens. —GLENN STEWART, SANTA CRUZ PREDATORY BIRD RESEARCH GROUP

A Merlin lands on what could be a dangerous perch. Larger birds in particular are electro-cuted when they touch grounded and live wires simultaneously. —NICK DUNLOP

7

Current Falcon Threats

Human activity continues to affect all North American falcon species both directly and indirectly on local, regional, and continental scales. Falcons continue to be directly disturbed, harassed, and killed, even during nesting, and untrained or poorly trained amateur and professional observers can create hazards to the birds. Mortalities and injuries are caused by collisions with vehicles, aircraft, and wind turbines, and electrocutions by power lines. Alteration of the environment is also destructive and longer lasting. Habitat is fragmented and lost to development, intensive agriculture, invasive species, and even wildfires. Environmental contaminants from past years persist, with current threats arising from newer compounds. Avian diseases have ravaged certain species. Finally, climate change can result in historical ranges becoming unsuitable for some species.

TARGETING OF FALCONS

Bounties as an incentive to kill raptors are gone, replaced by legal protections. Nevertheless, the concept of "good" and "bad" hawks persists among some people, and shooting, trapping, and harassing of birds of prey still occur. As recently as 2007 roller pigeon fanciers in Southern California were found to have been killing an estimated one thousand to two thousand hawks and falcons annually. Roller pigeons are prized by their owners because they have seizures and briefly roll, or tumble backward, in flight. However, this aberrant behavior also makes them targets for raptors, who zero in on apparently weak or wounded prey.

Members of roller pigeon clubs in seven states were targeted in a federal sting called Operation High Roller. The mostly Cooper's Hawks, Red-tailed Hawks, and Peregrine Falcons (but also American Kestrels, which don't prey on pigeons) were shot outright or trapped using pigeons as bait. Birds were then beaten with sticks or shot with pellet guns. One defendant admitted spraying the birds in the face with bleach and ammonia, another to suffocating them in plastic bags. News stories across the country asked that anyone seeing the boxlike hawk traps inform the U.S. Fish and Wildlife Service.

Defendants were charged with violating the Migratory Bird Treaty Act, and despite the maximum penalty of six months in prison, they were only given fines of $4,000 for their offenses.

Harassment of falcons may have dire consequences. Untrained biologists, observers, photographers, and falconers can pose a threat and even cause nest abandonment. Falcons are sensitive to commotion around the nest, and strict protocol has been established by professional field researchers for human activities during breeding to minimize interference. The welfare of the raptors is the primary concern. See pages 201–207 for detailed information on safely observing raptors in the field.

HUMAN-MADE HAZARDS

Power lines electrocute raptors, and the larger species that are able to touch conducting and ground wires simultaneously are most often killed or injured. In the United States electrocution isn't prevalent in falcons but was responsible for 25 percent of Golden Eagle deaths evaluated over a thirty-five-year period by the National Wildlife Health Center in Madison, Wisconsin. Especially hazardous are electrically conductive concrete and steel poles; these can be fatal when the bird touches a conductor when perched on a grounded cross arm. Electrocution also results when the bird touches two conductors simultaneously. Guidelines for modifying or retrofitting power lines and transformers were established in the 1970s and 1980s and updated in 2006. The power companies were responding not only to public concern over raptor fatalities but also to costly power outages—$34 million in 2005 in California alone—resulting from contact with wildlife. Wildfires may also result when the carcasses of electrocuted birds fall to the ground and ignite surrounding vegetation. Deregulation of the electric industry in the 1990s fragmented and possibly sidetracked efforts to reduce electrocution risks to raptors. Standardized procedures for assessing problems plus retrofitting technologies have since been developed, but their implementation varies between utilities. Cost-cutting measures by competitive companies often do not favor financial investment in modifying poles. And with the rising costs of energy, retrofitting millions of poles may not be a priority for the power utilities. It is a daunting task, with bulk transmission lines in 2001 stretching more than 500,000 miles (800,000 km) in the United States alone.

When a raptor is electrocuted, the power company is legally responsible, with fines that range from $5,000 to $500,000, plus imprisonment for up to two years. Raptors are protected under the Migratory Bird Treaty Act, Bald and Golden Eagle Protection Act, and Endangered Species Act, as well as by state laws. Punishment as incentive to prevent raptor electrocutions has rarely been carried out until fairly recently. In 1999, the U.S. Fish and Wild-life Service found Moon Lake Electrical Association in Utah and Colorado guilty of electrocuting seventeen raptors, including twelve Golden Eagles. The utility company was fined $100,000 in penalties with three years probation, and ordered to retrofit its utility lines to prevent electrocutions in the future. This was the first criminal prosecution of an electric utility. The U.S. Fish and Wildlife Service has stepped up efforts to reduce the raptor electrocution problem, and other utilities will probably incur hefty fines.

Utility poles are everywhere, and in the open, treeless terrain that is falcon country, they are especially favored by Prairie Falcons and Gyrfalcons as the best perches in the area for hunting and resting. Retrofitting power poles with insulation was found to be more effective that installing perch guards or alternative perches. Inexpensive polymer caps to fit over the dangerous lines are easy to install. Power companies like Idaho Power—an industry pioneer in research and retrofitting utility poles since the 1970s—began concentrating their retrofitting efforts in areas of high raptor density, such as the Snake River Birds of Prey National Conservation Area. Research in design should ensure that all new power lines are raptor-friendly, and those being replaced,

Inexpensive plastic perch guards are usually effective at preventing raptors from landing and nesting on power poles. —KATE DAVIS

such as the wooden poles (which are only functional for thirty to sixty years), must use technology to reduce electrocutions. Raptor-safe standards are available from the Avian Power Line Interaction Committee (APLIC).

Collisions with the power lines themselves are still a source of mortality. When a falcon is concentrating on hunting or is in a territorial dispute, lines may not be easily seen or avoided. Birds with high wing loading and rapid flight have the highest risk of power line collision. Obviously, underground cables are the safest, but conspicuous marking of overhead lines makes them more visible to flying raptors. Markers include spinning disks, colored spheres, streamers, and spiral PVC markers. Power lines along the leading lines of migratory routes and near barriers like cliffs that force birds to fly over them are particularly dangerous. Power companies may take into account topographical and climatic (wind) conditions that put raptors at greater risk when installing utility structures. Consumers can help by encouraging power providers to be environmentally concerned and active, and by reporting any incidents involving power lines and wildlife to authorities.

Communication towers for radio, television, emergency broadcast, and cellular phones kill an estimated four to five million birds each year, especially nocturnal migrant songbirds on nights of low cloud cover or fog. Birds are attracted to lights, especially on the taller towers, and they become disoriented and circle the structure; they may collide with the tower, guy wires, or other birds, or may collapse to the ground in exhaustion. With the recent craze for cellular phones and digital television, as many as ten thousand new towers are built every year. These unnatural obstructions certainly kill raptors as well, but probably not in especially high numbers.

The many hazards associated with roads often prove fatal for falcons. Roadways may be the only strips of land without vegetation in an area, making them especially appealing to open country falcons, which might be drawn in while migrating. In the winter, rodents attracted to the pavement by heat and road salt provide a prey source. Power and telephone poles along road routes also make hunting and roosting perches. These attractions increase the chances of falcons colliding with vehicles. Wire fences along roads may create additional collision hazards. Although falcons eat live prey, some raptors are carrion feeders and can be attracted by roadkill. Merlins and Prairie Falcons have been observed using moving traffic as a cover in prey-ambush flights, a potentially dangerous tactic. Nesting boxes for American Kestrels have been attached to interstate highway signs in the Midwest, and surprisingly fledgling mortality is not especially high. Perhaps being raised with traffic noise causes the fledglings to instinctively avoid it and fly in the other direction.

Collisions with aircraft are usually fatal for birds but also can be costly in terms of damage to the aircraft and danger to crew members and passengers. Wildlife collisions cost U.S. civil and military aviation well over $600 million

a year. Of the bird strikes reported from 1990 to 2007, 17 percent involved raptors. The Bird Strike Committee USA was formed in 1991 to address these issues, reduce wildlife hazards, and coordinate efforts with organizations in other countries. The Bird/Wildlife Aircraft Strike Hazard Team is a division of the U.S. Air Force with a similar objective. In 2006, the team began testing a radar system at Dover Air Force Base in Delaware that it hopes will prevent bird strikes. The Merlin Avian Radar System is able to detect wildlife on the ground and in the surrounding airspace in real time and 3D. It can alert pilots to nearby flocks of birds; it will also compile data on bird movement patterns. This technology could be helpful for commercial airports. Bird collisions may also be reduced by keeping airstrips free of cover for small prey animals by mowing, and by removing perches that raptors may favor for hunting and resting.

WIND FARMS

With the movement away from fossil fuels and toward clean energy sources, North America is seeing unprecedented growth in wind power. At just four to six cents per kilowatt-hour (compared to eleven cents for coal in California, for example), wind is one of the lowest-priced renewable energy technologies available. In the United States, energy generated by wind grew by 45 percent in 2007, and Mexico's ambitious projects La Venta II and La Venta III are generating electricity regionally.

Wind energy is touted as an ecologically friendly solution to our energy problems. Unfortunately, between habitat loss and collisions with turbines, the potential impacts on wildlife could be devastating. Because wind farms rely on high average wind speeds, they are located in open and exposed terrain, which is also ideal falcon habitat. Towers and rotors can reach heights of over 400 feet (120 meters). Wind farms are often built on ridgelines over and near breeding cliffs and on migration and local flight paths. Direct effects are collisions with the actual turbine blades and the associated structures of guy cables, power lines, and meteorological masts. Birds are unable to see the

A wind farm in Northern Colorado. —ROB PALMER

spinning blades (like humans can't see the spinning propellers on aircraft), a danger Shawn Smallwodd calls "motion smear." Displacement occurs when raptors avoid the site during construction and operation, and access roads and power stations result in habitat loss. Wind farms create a barrier effect when birds change their migration or daily flight path, which may increase their energy expenditure.

One of the first wind farms in the United States and largest in the world is Altamont Pass Wind Resources Area in central California, with over six thousand turbines located on 50 square miles (130 sq. km). A five-year study by biologists for the California Energy Commission documented high numbers of bird kills, as many as 4,700 a year, with nearly one-third of them raptors. A 1992 study found Red-tailed Hawk fatalities making up 36 percent, American Kestrels at 13 percent, and Golden Eagles at 11 percent, or as many as seventy-five eagles a year. Environmental groups called for replacement of the obsolete towers with fewer, taller turbines and slower-spinning blades. In 2005 the Alameda County Board of Supervisors passed a plan for Altamont Pass. New, safer towers will be placed on the leeward sides of hills, away from soaring birds rising on the windward side. In addition, some of the turbines are shut down during critical bird migration times. Conservationists hope that new wind farms will not be built in sensitive bird areas, and that new generators will be designed and operated to prevent or greatly reduce bird fatalities.

HABITAT LOSS

Raptors are negatively affected in indirect ways by other factors, and in ways that are difficult to undo. Whereas birds may be able to see the harmful result of a direct conflict with humans and learn to avoid it, the indirect effects are difficult for them to detect and evade or habituate to. A wide-ranging and devastating indirect impact to wildlife is the alteration of their environments through human use. Worldwide deteriorations have occurred in all major ecosystems. Invasive species cause a decline in habitat quality, and roads, power lines, mining, and logging degrade habitat. What was once an expanse of prairie is suddenly an industrial park or housing development, or is plowed for agriculture. When formerly unbroken natural expanses are dotted with development and divided by human growth, habitat is fragmented. Fragmentation leads to isolated populations, which can lead to a lack of genetic diversity. It also may cause an edge effect, in which harmful effects of predation, parasites, and adverse weather conditions are more likely to penetrate a small patch of habitat versus a vast, unaltered patch; the edge effect, however, is species specific and may ultimately benefit certain individuals. Falcons tend to be open country and wide-ranging birds, so the problems of forest loss do

Tundra habitat in the far north is the breeding grounds of Gyrfalcons. —ROB PALMER

not immediately affect them. However, changes in forest cover may affect the life cycles of their prey. In the last century land use has shifted to intensive agriculture and concentrated grazing, which does not favor biodiversity. The recent demand for biofuels has contributed to high grain prices; this in turn is causing millions of acres of prairie and wetlands to be converted for agriculture. Oil and gas development further transforms the natural environment, and all native species suffer as a result.

PESTICIDES

Environmental contaminants continue to have adverse effects on falcons, with more pesticides being used than ever before. Hazards to birds may be acute, with a sudden, short exposure to high levels of a contaminant that results in death, sometimes within thirty minutes. Chronic exposure to lower levels may also be lethal. Contaminants can lead to a weakened condition with impaired vision and reaction time. Reproductive failure and behavioral abnormalities are more difficult to assess, as is connecting these problems to pesticides.

DDT is a persistent organochlorine, and widespread use in the past continues to affect falcons and other birds such as pelicans. Eggshell thinning still occurs in Aplomado Falcons breeding in Mexico. The pesticide has an extensive half-life; how long it persists depends on the substrate of air, water, or soil. Despite DDT being banned in the United States and Canada in the early 1970s, it continued to be used in Mexico and the Central and South American countries where many North American falcon species and their prey spend the winter. However, recent evidence has shown encouraging signs that DDT is no longer in use in Latin America; migrant Peregrines that have wintered there are trapped in huge numbers at Padre Island, Texas, and tested for the DDT breakdown chemical DDE. Blood concentrations of DDE dropped gradually between 1978 and 1994, and had declined dramatically by 2004.

Pesticide alternatives for DDT, such as organophosphates, were introduced in the 1960s and 1970s and still pose a threat today. Although not as persistent as organochlorines, they are extremely toxic chemicals that are regularly used for agricultural and domestic (lawn and garden) pest control. Organophosphates affect the nervous systems of invertebrates and vertebrates; predators are killed through direct exposure, or indirectly via secondary poisoning from eating contaminated animals. It may take as long as five days for death to occur. Brian Woodbridge and colleagues discovered nearly six thousand dead Swainson's Hawks on their wintering grounds in 1995 and 1996 at Las Pampas, Argentina. Approximately twenty thousand Swainson's Hawks, or 8 percent of the world's population, were killed just that winter. The hawks had eaten grasshoppers sprayed with the organophosphate monocrotophos. The raptors also followed the spraying tractors, eating insects that were stirred up, and later ingested the poison by preening their contaminated feathers. The pesticide can enter the water supply through runoff, contaminating water that birds use for bathing and drinking, not to mention aquifers used by humans.

A second type of pesticide used to replace DDT is the group of carbamate insecticides, which can kill exposed birds within a few hours. The Environmental Protection Agency states that carbofuran has probably killed more birds than any other pesticide in the United States, perhaps two million a year, and more than one hundred species over thirty years. The U.S. Fish and Wildlife Service stated, "There are no known conditions under which carbofuran can be used without killing migratory birds." Sold as a liquid or solid, a single ingested granule is fatal, and it has killed raptors from eagles to kestrels; secondary exposure may also be deadly. In 1999, a farmer in Illinois was convicted of deliberately poisoning his small winter wheat field, where twenty-seven thousand bird carcasses were discovered (mostly blackbirds, grackles, cowbirds, and Horned Larks). Granular carbofuran was phased out

In flight, a male American Kestrel displays his striking gray and red colors along with white spots on the black wing feathers. —ROB PALMER

from use in the United States starting in 1991 and banned in Canada in 1998. As of 2006, the Environmental Protection Agency has proposed its complete ban in the United States.

Other pest control chemicals causing secondary poisoning and raptor fatalities are rodenticides, commonly known as rat poison; these are anticoagulants that cause hemorrhaging and neurological and cardiopulmonary damage when ingested. After a ten-year evaluation of rodenticides, the Environmental Protection Agency announced in May 2008 its decision to strictly control their use by removing the most toxic forms from the market and replacing them with less dangerous varieties. Ironically, raptors may be better at keeping rodents in check than the poisons themselves. American Kestrels catch huge numbers of mice and voles, and Prairie Falcons prey on pocket gophers and ground squirrels—all targets of poisoning campaigns.

OTHER CONTAMINANTS

Additional human-generated effects on wildlife include contamination from elements such as lead, mercury, zinc, selenium, and cadmium. All of these occur naturally, but human activities release them into the environment at levels that can cause reproductive failure, behavioral changes, and even adult mortality in raptors. Industrial processes, fossil fuel combustion, mining, fertilizers, smelter emissions, and sewage sludge all contribute to the problem. As with insecticides and rodenticides, raptors are affected through secondary poisoning after feeding on contaminated prey.

PCBs and PBDEs are also global contaminants. They are absorbed in the fat of animals and accumulate in increasing concentrations as they move up the food chain. PCBs (polychlorinated biphenyls) were used in plastic and paint manufacturing and as insulation in electrical transformers. Their manufacture was discontinued in the United States in 1978, but because they are inert and stable when heated, they remain in the environment for a long time after they are discarded. Global winds also bring banned chemicals to North America from countries where they remain in use. Some of the highest levels of PCB contamination for any animal have been found in eagles and falcons. PBDEs (polybrominated diphenyl ethers)—a group of flame retardants found in most plastics as well as foams and textiles—are also present at high concentrations. PBDEs don't bind chemically with plastic, so they continuously leach out of the product into the environment. Both PBCs and PBDEs are insidious; instead of seeing a direct cause and effect on falcons, as with DDT, endocrine levels, and hence behavior, are subtly altered. Immediate mortality rarely occurs, but thyroid and pituitary changes may result in low reproductive success (eggshell thinning, decreased parental attentiveness) and problems with immune system function. These disruptions may be difficult to assess but are often deadly in the long run.

Lead can also enter the diets of falcons in a much more direct way. Falcons are often poisoned by eating the lead pellets of ammunition that remain embedded in prey animals that have been shot but not killed. When a falcon ingests even one pellet, it may take only a week before the absorption of hazardous levels of lead causes behavioral changes. Symptoms are disorientation and bright green diarrhea staining the feathers around the vent (cloaca); mortality may not occur for several weeks. Peregrines and Prairie Falcons have been poisoned by lead shot, and it is considered a serious threat for Aplomado Falcons because of their preference for game birds such as quail and doves. Lead shot is also deadly to waterfowl that ingest spent shotgun pellets. Lead ammunition was banned for waterfowl hunting in the United States in 1991; Canada banned it on waterways in 1997 and then nationwide in 1999 (except for woodcocks, pigeons, and doves). A recent California state law banning the use of all lead ammunition in the range of California Condors will be of great assistance in the recovery of the species and certainly will benefit other raptors, like Golden Eagles and Turkey Vultures.

There are several methods for collecting information on the levels of pesticides and other contaminants present in raptors. The first is analysis of the eggs—either those that remain in the nest without hatching or a viable egg from a nest, preferably about one or two weeks into incubation. The levels at which chemical toxicity causes eggshell thinning varies among species (different levels for eagles and falcons, for example). A second method of testing involves taking blood plasma samples, from both adults and chicks if possible. A third method for gathering information involves analyzing liver, kidney, and brain tissue to assess contaminant levels in dead birds. Feathers may also be analyzed for levels of metals such as mercury, zinc, lead, and selenium. Future studies in birds may lead to changes in uses of chemicals and dangerous compounds that also affect humans.

DISEASE AND CLIMATE CHANGE

Avian diseases have always killed raptors, and recently West Nile virus has been deadly. Transmitted by mosquitoes, the virus causes encephalitis, an inflammation of the spinal cord and brain that can be fatal. West Nile virus swept across the country in just five years after the first infections were recorded in the New York city area in 1999. Jays and crows have been the hardest hit; Great Horned Owls and Red-tailed Hawks have also been killed in high numbers. Of the falcons, all but the Aplomado Falcon have been infected. The disease practically wiped out some captive bird centers, and avian vaccinations have since been developed based on vaccinations used on horses. For wild bird populations, the disease will run its course and resistant individuals will survive, but the health effects on birds and humans are still a concern.

One factor allowing West Nile virus to become widespread so quickly is climate change. Rising temperatures have allowed mosquito populations to explode, and with them mosquito-borne diseases like West Nile virus. Human activities are changing the climate by increasing the amount of carbon dioxide in the atmosphere, along with other greenhouse gases like methane, nitrous oxide, ozone, and halocarbons. Three-quarters of CO_2 is generated through the burning of fossil fuels, and the remaining increase is due to shifts in land use, primarily deforestation. While the majority of scientists believe that human activity has contributed to global warming, there is no doubt that we are in a warming cycle, whether human caused or not. The environmental impacts resulting from climate change are currently being determined and examined. Birds have been especially fitting subjects in studies discerning the effects of climate change on wildlife (as well as humankind). Long-term datasets are available for many bird species, and direct and indirect changes in bird behavior are readily observed by researchers.

Processes such as timing of migration and breeding have been affected by a warming climate. Geographic shifts in range and even population size have

THE RAPTOR CENTER, UNIVERSITY OF MINNESOTA

The Raptor Center at the University of Minnesota has been a leader in avian medicine for more than thirty years. Established in 1974 as part of the University Minnesota College of Veterinary Medicine, the center has been instrumental in developing many avian surgical practices now used throughout the world. And it all started with four baby owls.

In the early 1970s, Gary Duke, a faculty member at the University of Minnesota College of Medicine, was conducting research on the digestion of grain-eating turkeys when one of his students brought him four baby Great Horned Owls. Duke, while enamored with the owlets, also saw an opportunity to expand his digestion studies into carnivorous birds. Pat Redig, one of Duke's students and a falconer, offered to care for the growing number of raptors acquired for the study. In 1974, the two men moved their raptor facility into a hall on the campus.

Redig soon began rehabilitating and releasing some of the study birds and in the process discovered new methods of bird anesthesia and orthopedic surgery. In 1981, he published *Medical Management of Birds of Prey*, which is in its third edition and still considered one of the definitive texts for avian veterinarian medicine. Redig, along with Bud Tordoff of the Bell Museum of Natural History, also started the Midwest Peregrine Falcon Restoration Project, one of many such projects began in the United States during this time for the purpose of releasing captive-bred Peregrine Falcons into the wild.

The Raptor Center is still on the cutting edge of avian veterinarian medicine. Researchers there are working on a species-specific vaccine for West Nile virus, which in 2002 killed thousands of raptors in the Midwest. Lori Arent, an assistant director at the center, published *Raptors in Captivity: A Guide to Care and Management*, required reading for raptor rehabilitators and educators. Every year the center admits more than 750 birds, which are rehabilitated and used for training veterinarians from around the world. Their outreach education program also reaches more than 240,000 people annually with the message of conservation of wild raptors and their natural world.

been detected since the beginning of the last part of the twentieth century. Most vulnerable are species that tolerate only a narrow range of temperatures, have low population numbers, are geographically isolated, or are highly specialized (as opposed to being a generalist). Birds might run the gamut of what have been called winners and losers in the time of climate change. Some species may adjust smoothly, or even benefit, while others may suffer greatly.

Compelling evidence already points to changes in the timing of many behaviors associated with weather and climate. The term *phenology* refers to the study of regularly occurring biological events or seasonal activities. Research in phenology indicates that, along with many other living organisms, some birds are doing things earlier in the seasons, and doing them differently, than they ever have before. Already, recent mild winters have had an effect on Prairie Falcons breeding in Idaho. Those Prairie Falcons that spend the winter closer to the breeding grounds may displace the long-distance migrants that

A male American Kestrel. —ROB PALMER

remain on the wintering grounds longer and arrive on the breeding grounds later in the spring. Researchers call it a microevolutionary change; in this case, the change favors individuals that travel shorter distances or remain near the breeding grounds over the winter. This behavior may also affect Peregrines wintering in the Southern Hemisphere; by using day length as a cue to leave, they may arrive later in the breeding grounds in the Northern Hemisphere than short-distance migrant Peregrines, which may be influenced to begin nesting by environmental cues other than day length. Additionally, a wide variety of species are expanding their ranges into areas that were presumably once too cold, with some birds moving farther north in the Northern Hemisphere, and others moving uphill to higher elevations.

Evidence indicates that some raptors have been affected by the early stages of climate change, with changes in their nesting chronology, clutch and egg sizes, and overall breeding success. The timing of food supply and nestling demand is critical. Ideally, the most difficult activities should coincide with optimal conditions of food abundance, but this doesn't always happen now. Egg-laying dates for many raptors are now occurring earlier in the season, and survival rates may be lower than in previous years. Alterations in wintering and breeding population sizes and distributions have also been observed. These effects may be compounded by habitat fragmentation, degradation, and loss. Competition from other species that were previously not present is another factor.

Extreme random weather events have become more frequent. Intense storms, heat waves, cold spells, flooding, and droughts are commonplace, and the impacts are more critical to smaller-bodied birds than larger-bodied. Hot weather and droughts have contributed to devastating outbreaks of spruce budworms and mountain pine beetles in the United States and Canada. Up to 80 percent of the pine forests of British Columbia may be dead by 2013 because of the pine beetle. Dead trees will rot or burn, further contributing to greenhouse gases in the atmosphere. And songbirds that breed in these forests may decline, affecting the availability of prey for falcons. Climate change continues to be a controversial topic, but one with wide-ranging impacts that may drastically affect global biodiversity.

A Peregine Falcon races through a flock of American Advocets. Peregines feed primarily on birds, usually caught in flight. —NICK DUNLOP

Finale

Current hazards to falcons are clearly numerous and complex, and the solutions require immediate and lasting action. Young people today are aware of global threats, but may have an increasing "disconnect" with their natural world, as described by Richard Louv. He coined the term "nature-deficit disorder" in his 2005 book *Last Child in the Woods*, and pointed out that children today are far less likely to play outdoors than a generation ago. Reasons include the up to forty hours a week "screen time" in front of the computer and television, less access to natural areas, and fears of stranger-danger leading to "virtual protective house arrest." However, he has found that children who spend time in nature have greatly reduced health problems, less attention deficit disorder, and increased problem-solving ability. Appreciation of the natural world may lead them to become involved in conservation issues as adults.

Providing high-quality education to youngsters has been the goal of scores of raptor organizations across the continent. To see a live falcon up close (or at any distance) may be an unforgettable experience, inspiring a lifelong awareness of raptors. This may be especially effective if the participants are actively involved, learning for themselves, thinking through a situation, and coming to a conclusion. As educators, the challenge is to deliver a message in a way that is richer and more entertaining. Methods to be avoided are melodramatic and exploitative depictions of birds of prey. For better or worse, terms like "infotainment" and "edutainment" are entering the vocabulary. Rather than jargon and the commercialization of education, a better approach would be instilling curiosity, interest, and respect for the natural world. These qualities have always been important, and may be more crucial now than ever.

Researchers agree that without raptor education for the public, their projects would be difficult to fund; public support and approval is critical. In successful environmental education, positive attitudes toward raptors are fostered in children and adults through effective communication skills for a new age.

Now is an exciting (and frightening) time to be a researcher, and all of the effects humans will have on falcons remain to be seen. A sense of urgency prevails, with significant studies to be conducted and decisions to be made.

An optimistic outlook would allow hope that falcons, icons of the efforts to preserve species, will adapt and thrive.

Falcons exemplify a lifestyle that humans can't help but admire. Their astonishing prowess in mastering the skies, predatory skills, and "noble" appearance set falcons apart from other raptors. An American Kestrel will hover in the breeze, flicks of the wings keeping it steady over a patch of prairie. Their raucous family groups are a common sight in the late summer, perched on fences with young begging and testing their flying skills. A Merlin can cause a flock of blackbirds to explode, a single bird selected for a chase. The smaller aggressor mobbing the migrating Golden Eagle is probably a brazen, persistent Merlin.

The desert denizen making a comeback is the Aplomado Falcon, dashing through the brush after a bird, tight through the vegetation and determined. Perched on a yucca, the colorful Aplomado displays striking slate gray and rufous plumage, with a bold black and white head pattern and belly band. A Prairie Falcon's *kak-kak-kak* breaks the silence of the western bluff, but trying to locate the source on the sandy cliff face can be a challenge because

Students in Salmon, Idaho, meet a live raptor in their classroom. —IDAHO FISH AND GAME

of the bird's cryptic brown coloration. Courtship flight aerobatics are often breathtaking, seeming to defy what our common sense would feel is safe.

A Peregrine roll and stoop from the clouds is wondrous, pursuing the most difficult of quarries—that of birds in the air. At fledging time, the antics of the young at play can be mischievous, dropping and catching sticks in flight, and chasing siblings, parents, and anything else that enters their airspace. The flight of a Gyrfalcon past a pond makes the ducks tense up, hold tight, and then finally make a break. A sight that can be etched in a mind forever is the visage of a large falcon in a blizzard on a rocky outcrop, fluffed out and comfortable, feet covered with long belly feathers, waiting out the storm.

By observing falcons going about their lives in the wild, many humans run the risk of becoming addicted falconphiles. Perhaps it's envy, and it's certainly admiration. Air is the element for a falcon. Even with top technological advances in aircraft, humans can never attain their flight skills—dropping from the sky at unbelievable speeds, shifting gears with minute wing and tail adjustments, turning on a dime, braking, and colliding with their prey in a blast of feathers. *Speed.* Many revere these falcons that bring them joy, and a sense of awe and wonder and splendor.

American Kestrel
Falco sparverius

Length: *male:* 8 to 10 inches (22 to 27 centimeters); *female:* 9 to 12 inches (23 to 31 centimeters)

Wingspan: *male:* 20 to 22 inches (51 to 56 centimeters); *female:* 22 to 24 inches (57 to 61 centimeters)

Weight: *male:* 2 to 5 ounces (80 to 143 grams); *female:* 3 to 6 ounces (86 to 165 grams)

Description: The colorful, robin-sized American Kestrel is the smallest falcon in North America. Ornithologist William Brewster described it in 1925 as "most light-hearted and frolicsome." This is the only falcon in North America with a reddish back and tail. Male and female are sexually dimorphic; not only is the female slightly larger, but the two sexes have separate plumages even as youngsters, which is uncommon for raptors. Males have slate gray "shoulders," or wing coverts, and a solid rufous tail with a black band at the tip. The female has a rufous back and tail, and the tail is barred. Both sexes have black malar stripes and gray caps with a rufous spot on the top of the head. When perching the wingtips end far short of the tail tip. The female averages about 10 percent heavier than the male. The immature bird looks like an adult, but with more streaking below. The skin of the legs, eye ring, and cere are pale yellow in the young bird, turning brighter yellow and even orange in the adult male. Plumage varies to some degree over the bird's large geographic range.

Range: The most widespread North American falcons, American Kestrels inhabit central Alaska from north of the Arctic Circle to Canada, the United States, Mexico, and Central America, and most of South America to Tierra del Fuego (they are absent from the Brazilian coast and Amazon Basin).

Habitat: Kestrels live in the open country of farmland, pasture, parkland, orchard, and field, plus desert and prairie. Ideal habitats have perches, prey, and nest sites. These birds are absent from dense forest. Kestrels often associate with areas of human activity, such as city parks, woodlots, and farms. Females winter in more open habitats, and may exclude males, which tend to winter in denser cover. Kestrels often return to their wintering ground year after year, defending it like a breeding territory. American Kestrels are thought to be the most common diurnal raptors in their range; their Old World counterpart, Common Kestrels (*Falco tinnunculus*), are considered, along with the Black Kite, to be the most numerous diurnal raptors worldwide.

Behavior: Kestrels are conspicuous and loud. They are often seen perched out in the open on telephone lines, bare tree limbs, and posts. They frequently bob their tails and pump their heads up and down, especially when landing or when excited. The head bob also allows them to use motion parallax to better determine distance when

A male American Kestrel boasts a buffy chest and slate gray scapulars. —KATE DAVIS

A female American Kestrel displays the rufous scapulars and tail with barring. Young have the same plumage as their adult counterparts, but with more streaking below. —ROB PALMER

The colorful male American Kestrel has slate gray wing coverts and a solid red tail with a terminal black bar. —ROB PALMER

observing prey, as well as predators—larger raptors may prey on them. Kestrels are primarily "sit-and-wait" hunters, watching from a perch for a meal to pass by. They feed mostly on prey on the ground, such as large insects (grasshoppers, crickets, and beetles) and rodents (mice and voles). Kestrels tend to dive feetfirst at insects and headfirst at mammalian prey. Males are more likely to kill small birds, particularly in the winter. Kestrels may hunt insects on foot; other prey includes amphibians and—especially in deserts—small reptiles. They tend to hover while hunting more than other raptors do.

Siblings may hunt as social groups, and gatherings of up to twenty juveniles and adults may hunt together in the fall. This behavior may be imitative rather than cooperative, with youngsters watching and copying the successful adult hunters. They are also known to follow farm equipment and cattle, preying on flushed insects, birds, and mammals. Kestrels roost in cavities or in dense vegetation to avoid detection by nocturnal predators.

Flight: In flight the wings curve gradually backward, without harsh angles, and wingtips are rounded. A slightly pinched-in area forms where the wings meet the body. Kestrels glide more than most other falcons. Their small size makes them appear delicate and buoyant. They often hover with rapidly beating wings, facing into the wind, head steady as they scan the ground below. Other times they hover with quivering wingtips, seemingly motionless, before swooping down to a different location. They are more likely to hover in moderate breezes than in still air or harsh winds.

Breeding: Woodpecker holes or natural cavities in trees are favored nest sites; abandoned magpie nests, which are roofed over, may also be used. Kestrels occasionally nest in the eaves of buildings and crevices in rocks, cliffs, or dirt banks. Courtship displays include the "dive-display," in which the male climbs and calls three to five sharp *killy* notes and then descends. The "flutter-glide," a slow flight with quick wing beats, is performed by both sexes. The male and female also allopreen during courtship and nesting.

It has been suggested that American Kestrels may have originally used an open nest and not a closed cavity for breeding. The young defecate forcefully away from the center of the nest, and the eggs are cryptically colored and oval—not the typical traits of a cavity nester. The American Kestrel is also thought to be the most recently evolved of all of the kestrels.

Typically, 4 to 5, and sometimes 6, eggs are laid. The female performs most of the incubation duties, and eggs hatch at 28 to 31 days. The young fledge at 28 to 31 days, and may rely on their parents for food for up to a month.

Vocalizations: They are vocal year-round, especially during the breeding season. The call is a series of five or more sharp *kleee* notes, often described as *killy, killy, killy*. They also make an excited chittering, especially between pairs. Like all falcons, the young birds hiss, with vocalizations resembling those of adults at 16 days of age.

American Kestrel habitat with nest box installed in an open riparian area. —KATE DAVIS

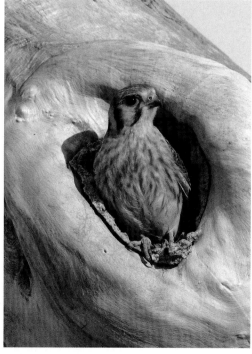

A male American Kestrel holds a mouse with one foot. Rodents and insects are major parts of their diet, but males tend to catch more prey birds than females, especially over the winter. —ROB PALMER

A female American Kestrel checks out her surroundings from a cavity nest. She has more streaking on the breast compared to the male. —ROB PALMER

Movement: American Kestrels vary from sedentary year-round residents to highly migratory. Northern populations migrate to the southern United States and into Mexico and Central America. These northern birds exhibit leapfrog migration, passing over less migratory and resident birds to end up farther south in the winter. Kestrels may migrate in small groups of three or four birds, or in loose flocks of up to ten. Their flight is usually fast and at low altitude with active wing beats. Juveniles precede adults in fall migration, and males return to breeding grounds first in the spring. Northern birds migrate south on a regular schedule each year, perhaps as a result of photoperiod, the shortening autumn days, rather than sudden harsh weather. Studies indicate that departure is timed exactly with the last portion of flight-feather molt. Females molt early, during nesting; juveniles have all of their feathers when they leave the nest. Both leave the breeding grounds before the males, which complete their molt later.

Conservation: The Kestrel population may be restricted in certain areas by the availability of nesting sites. Current research (Raptor Population Index) indicates declines of the American Kestrel across much of North America, with significant population drops in the eastern half, especially along the coast. Loss of cavity-providing trees, competition with other cavity nesters like the abundant European Starling, and predation by Cooper's Hawks that are habituated to hunting at nest boxes are all cited as possible reasons. Loss of grassland habitats and West Nile virus may also contribute, and current drought is thought to be a key factor in the West. The definitive answer is still unknown, but it may be a variety of local and regional factors.

Cooper's Hawks aside, human-made nest boxes have greatly benefited American Kestrels in many parts of the country. Breeding pairs will use these artificial nesting sites, and there are several programs across the country to install and monitor the boxes. A box with the proper dimensions and hole size is placed overlooking a hunting area with good perches nearby. If a breeding pair discovers it, a box may be occupied year after year. One program in the Midwest attaches the nest boxes to the backs of highway signs. See pages 208–209 for instructions on how to build a Kestrel nest box.

Science and research have greatly benefited from studying captive American Kestrels. David Bird of McGill University in Montreal has bred more than 5,000 Kestrels over the past thirty years; his work has made key contributions to studies with kestrels, including behavior, environmental toxicology, disease, embryonic growth, and effects of electromagnetic fields associated with power lines.

Subspecies in North America: Seventeen subspecies are recognized in North, Central, and South America, with three of them occurring in North America:

F. s. sparverius: The nominant subspecies; it occurs over most of North America.

F. s. paulus: Occurs in the southeastern United States from Louisiana east to Florida and South Carolina. A small bird, it tends to have less spotting and streaking than *sparverius.*

F. s. peninsularis: Resident of southern Baja California, Mexico; smaller and paler than *sparverius*, with less prominent malar stripes.

This male American Kestrel is about to land. Note the rusty breast and black spotting. Kestrels nearly always bob their tails up and down when they land.
—ROB PALMER

A young male American Kestrel launches from the cavity nest in a tree. The young will fledge at a month old and rely on their parents for food for up to another month. —ROB PALMER

Food is transferred between a mated pair of American Kestrels. During courtship the females beg for food like youngsters. —ROB PALMER

Etymology: American Kestrels were formerly called Sparrowhawks, a misnomer given by pioneers who mistook them for the true hawks of the Old World, the accipiters. *Kestrel* indicates that it is a falcon; there are thirteen kestrel species around the world. *Falco* is the genus of the true falcons; *sparverius* is Latin for "pertaining to a sparrow."

Tidbit: With their forward-facing eyes that allow for binocular vision, raptors have a blind spot behind them. Both sexes of American Kestrels have two black spots near the back of the head. These plumage patterns are called ocelli and are a type of "deflective" coloration. The ocelli may act as "false eyes" because they may look like a face, with buff or white surrounding what look like black pupils, and a gray "beak" in between. The Northern Pygmy-owl has a similar color pattern on the back of its head. The ocelli have been described as "misrepresenting the posture" of the kestrel or owl. False eyes may deceive an enemy or thief into thinking the falcon is looking right at them so that the element of surprise is gone. The ocelli may signal that the bird is "unprofitable prey." This is especially true if the Kestrel is bent over, plucking and eating a bird, for example; the ocelli are in plain view. Another theory is that the false eyes help keep mobbing passerines at a distance. A third, and somewhat romantic, speculation suggests that the false eyes strengthen pair bonding between mates, because they appear to be constantly gazing at each other.

A trained female American Kestrel comes in for a reward. —ROB PALMER

The ocelli, or false eyes, of an American Kestrel can fool kleptoparasites. —KATE DAVIS

With a turn of the head the ocelli stand out. —KATE DAVIS

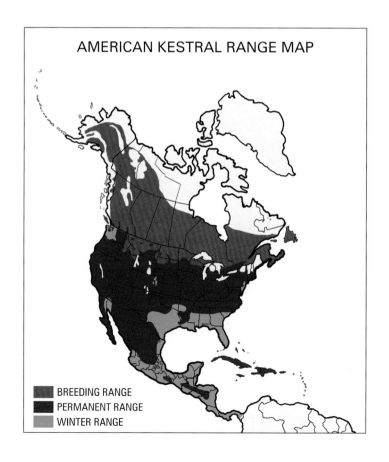

AMERICAN KESTRAL RANGE MAP

BREEDING RANGE
PERMANENT RANGE
WINTER RANGE

Merlin
Falco columbarius

Length: *male:* 9 to 11 inches (24 to 27 cm); *female:* 11 to 12 inches (28 to 30 cm)

Wingspan: *male:* 21 to 23 inches (53 to 58 cm); *female:* 24 to 27 inches (61 to 68 cm)

Weight: *male:* 5.6 to 6. ounces (160 to 170 grams); *female:* 7.8 to 8.5 ounces (220 to 240 grams)

Description: The Merlin is a small, stocky falcon, slightly larger than the more common American Kestrel. It appears completely dark when seen from a distance (except the Richardson's subspecies). The Merlin is comparatively short-winged for a falcon, with a long tail and deep chest. The male generally has blue gray or slate gray dorsal plumage, and the female and juvenile are brown; the three North American subspecies exhibit substantial color variation. The tail is dark with light bands. On a perched bird, the wingtips reach three-quarters down the length of the tail. The Merlin has streaked underparts with a white throat and faint malar stripes that are barely recognizable. Juveniles of both sexes are almost identical to the adult female, with slight color differences between the young male and female. Males differentiate at the first molt. The female is always larger than the male with no overlap in size between the sexes.

Range: Merlins breed in most of Canada and Alaska, the northern Great Plains, and the western United States where suitable habitat exists. They winter primarily in the western United States, with sporadic movements into the central and coastal states. Migrant Taiga Merlins move south into Mexico, Central America, and northern South America. They also winter in many northern towns and cities of the Inter-mountain West. Merlins are Holarctic, meaning they occur across the continents of the Northern Hemisphere.

Habitat: These falcons rely on open and semiopen habitats for hunting. They inhabit forest edges, fields, marshes, parkland, prairie, and tundra. They may winter at sea-shores and tidal flats and prey upon shorebirds. Large numbers of Merlins have taken up full-time residence in cities, especially in the north-central United States and Canadian provinces. Some winter in northern towns of the Intermountain West.

Behavior: Merlins are usually solitary and have been described as most often seen briefly, flying "away," often from a bird feeder. Their diet consists mostly of birds, pri-marily those that feed on or near the ground. A list of prey from 1893 names such birds as teal, snipe, swift, quail, various songbirds, and Eskimo Curlew, a species now extinct. Several studies of food habits show the House Sparrow and Bohemian Wax-wing as their preferred prey. Larger insects, small mammals, and even bats are also

Female Merlins are just a little bit larger, more stocky, and less likely to be perched in the open than the American Kestrel. —ROB PALMER

Note the size difference of this pair of Richardson's Merlins. The smaller male, with the slate gray plumage, perches above the female. —ROB PALMER

This magpie nest was used by a pair of Merlins. They rely largely on the nests of corvids, and those built by magpies are favored for the overhead dome. —ROB PALMER

eaten. Dragonflies are a major food item for the Taiga Merlin in migration. Younger birds especially will feed on rodents.

Dunne, Sibley, and Sutton describe the Merlin as "the Porsche Carrera of the falcon clan." They may hunt from a perch or cruise low to the ground using trees, shrubs, hills, and even houses and moving cars as cover before they dart out in dashing flight. Merlins may occasionally stoop on birds from moderate heights. Certain species that they pursue try to escape by outflying the falcon. Larks and waxwings fly swiftly in circles, higher and higher, resulting in the "ringing flight" that made Merlins so popular with the ladies of the court in medieval falconry days.

Merlins sometimes hunt using a "camouflage flight," bouncing through the air with wing beats and glides, which resembles the flight of a songbird or woodpecker. This often allows the Merlin to get close to its prey before it is recognized as a predator. If songbirds see a Merlin flying nearby, they freeze in place, often in awkward, stretched poses. The songbirds will resume feeding or singing only when they feel they are again safe.

Merlins may have a favored plucking post where they remove the wings, legs, feathers, and head of their avian prey before feeding. The Merlin is intolerant of other raptors. It brazenly harasses larger raptors throughout the year, not just during the breeding season, often chasing them for long distances.

Flight: These falcons will fly low in a burst of speed with powerful wing beats to catch birds in midair in a direct flight. The quick, forceful downstroke at the wrist is characteristic of this species. The wings are very angular and meet the body flush, without a pinched-in spot; wingtips are pointed. When not chasing prey, the Merlin can fly at an average flight speed of about 30 miles per hour.

Breeding: Merlins take over old nests of crows, magpies, and other corvids (members of the crow family), and may nest on the domed top of a chambered magpie nest rather than inside. They also use hawk nests. Shelterbelts—trees planted in the open as windbreaks—are favored for nesting and perching. Merlins rarely use the same nest two years in a row, but generally return to the same area. Merlins may nest on a rock ledge, with the female making the scrape or small depression in the substrate. They have been known to nest in tree cavities, and sometimes on the ground. An average of 4 eggs are laid; 3 to 6 may be present. Both sexes incubate, but the female handles the majority of the duties. The eggs hatch at 28 to 32 days. The male provides most of the food. The female will hunt when the young are about 3 weeks old, or perhaps wait until after they fledge. Young remain near the nest for up to 1 month following fledging, and depend on their parents for food. Up to 70 percent of Merlins die within their first year.

Vocalizations: They are usually silent, but vocalizations are more common during the breeding season. Both sexes give a *kek-kek-kek* call, with the male's voice being higher-pitched and more rapid than the female's. Adults also give a *chirr* call, and the female has a begging *pee-eh* call when she wants to be fed. Vocalizations resemble those of the larger falcons.

A Black Merlin pursues a starling. —ROB PALMER

Richardson's Merlins, like many raptors, may have a favorite plucking post. —NICK DUNLOP

A Merlin in a stoop. —ROB PALMER

Three newly fledged Richardson's Merlins perch in a tree. Their plumage is identical to that of adult females. Males become more gray at the one-year molt. —ROB PALMER

Movement: The three subspecies vary substantially in migration distances. The nominant Taiga or Boreal Merlin is the most migratory and might fly from Alaska and Northern Canada to the equator in South America. The Pacific Coast Black Merlin is somewhat sedentary, and the Richardson's Merlin is only partially migratory, with some individuals remaining in urban areas year-round. Females are the first to leave the breeding grounds. The Merlin migrates in typical active falcon flight. Most individuals breeding in eastern North America winter in the Caribbean Islands.

Conservation: Eggshell thinning due to the pesticide DDT affected Merlin population numbers before the chemical was banned in 1969 (Canada) and 1972 (U.S.). A study from 1971 found that in Canada and the Great Plains, Merlin reproductive rates had dropped as much as 30 percent from pre-1950s populations. Even with the ban on DDT, significant eggshell thinning was seen as late as 1988 on the Canadian prairies. The Merlin's overall status is probably no longer threatened by the contaminant. The Raptor Population Index 2008 reports that Merlin numbers increased in eastern North America starting in 1974, and in the West starting in the early 1980s. This trend has slowed since the late 1990s.

Subspecies in North America: The same species lives across the Northern Hemisphere, with ten subspecies recognized worldwide. The three North American subspecies perfectly display a plumage characteristic called Gloger's Rule: Merlins in humid areas are darker with heavier pigmentation than the birds inhabiting dry, arid environments.

F. c. columbarius: Known as the Taiga or Boreal Merlin, this species is the nominant race, inhabiting Alaska, northern Canada, and the western mountain states. It is the most migratory of the three subspecies, wintering as far south as northern South America. Its black tail usually has three light bands with a white band at the tip. Taiga Merlins may interbreed with the other two subspecies where the ranges overlap.

F. c. richardsoni: Also known as the Richardson's or Prairie Merlin, this bird is much paler than other subspecies, and males are light gray. It inhabits the prairies of Alberta, Saskatchewan, Montana, Wyoming, and the Dakotas. It winters in arid regions of the western United States and in northern Mexico. The dark tail has four light bands, with a white tip. It averages slightly larger and heavier than the other two subspecies.

F. c. suckleyi: Often referred to as the Black or Pacific Merlin, this is considered a Northwest Coastal forest bird of humid climates. The black tail has just one or two narrow bands. It inhabits southeast Alaska and British Columbia south to Washington State. Usually sedentary, some individuals venture into northern California (occasionally farther south) and the interior Northwest in migration.

Etymology: While they do eat pigeons, Merlins were formerly called Pigeon Hawks not because of their prey but because they are about the same size as pigeons and

An adult female or juvenile Taiga (Boreal) Merlin has three light tail bands and a white band at the tail tip. —NICK DUNLOP

This Black Merlin wintered near a dairy in central Nevada, an uncommon wintering ground for this subspecies. Note the single narrow tail band. —NICK DUNLOP

This male Richardson's Merlin perches on a stalk of mullein. —ROB PALMER

A female or juvenile Richardson's Merlin is an overall light brown. —ROB PALMER

resemble them in flight. In Latin, the species name *columbarius* means "pertaining to a dove (pigeon)." The name Merlin comes from *Esmerillon*, the Old French word for the European Merlin.

Tidbit: Many Merlin populations in North America have increased dramatically over the last several decades, due in large part to expanding urban landscapes and the banning of the pesticide DDT. Richardson's Merlins have adapted well to the cities of Canada and the Great Plains. Studies by Lynn Oliphant revealed a new tactic employed by this subspecies. With the planting of ornamental spruce trees, magpies and crows have become common city residents. Their abandoned nests provide the Merlin with a chance to breed in cities. Mountain ash and serviceberry, also planted as ornamentals, feed huge flocks of Bohemian Waxwings, a wintertime food supply for the Merlin. Plus, with resident House Sparrows and European Starlings to eat, many Merlins ceased migrating. These urban falcons seem to have adapted to humans in a very short time, and have benefited in a way not often seen in the raptor world.

The long legs and toes of a Merlin are well adapted for grabbing birds in the air.
—ROB PALMER

MERLIN RANGE MAPS

Taiga

Richardson's

Black

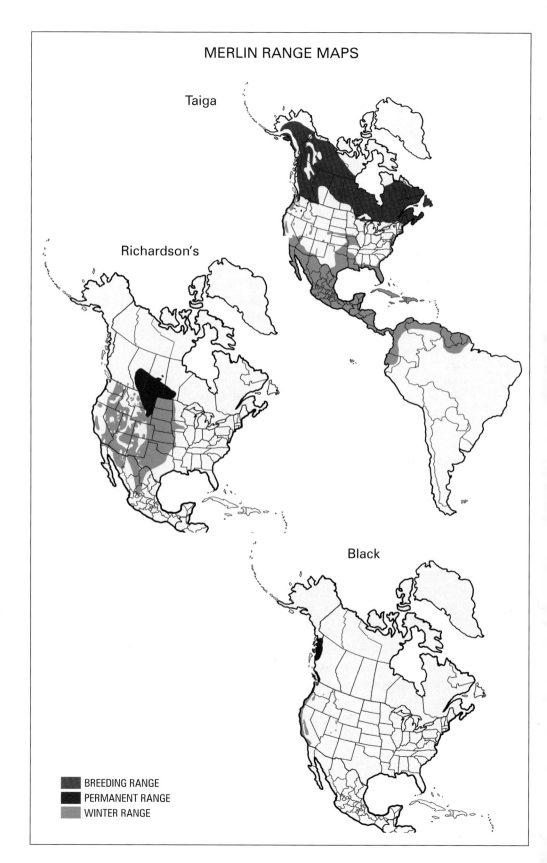

BREEDING RANGE
PERMANENT RANGE
WINTER RANGE

Aplomado Falcon
Falco femoralis

Length: *male:* 14 to 16 inches (35 to 39 cm); *female:* 16 to 18 inches (41 to 45 cm)

Wingspan: *male:* 31 to 33 inches (78 to 84 cm); *female:* 37 to 40 inches (93 to 102 cm)

Weight: *male:* 7.3 to 10.8 ounces (208 to 305 grams); *female:* 11 to 16.2 ounces (310 to 460 grams)

Description: The Aplomado Falcon is a colorful, medium-sized falcon. Its narrow wings reach three-quarters to the tip of the tail when perched. The light breast and rusty underparts are separated by a black belly band shaped like an hourglass; this marking may be referred to as a cumberbund. The black tail is long and narrow with thin, whitish bands. The Aplomado head is distinctive, with light cheeks and throat, a black eye stripe, a narrow malar stripe, and a creamy supercilliary line. This line extends to the back of the head, forming a V, which is set off by the dark crown. Both sexes have very similar plumage. The adult male has a clear white breast, and the female has thin breast streaks. The female may be as much as 45 percent heavier than the male but there can be substantial overlap between the sexes. Juvenal plumage is more rufous above, and the white upper breast is streaked with dark brown. The belly band is more complete than the adult's, and is dark brown with tawny streaking.

Range: In North America the Aplomado Falcon occurs in pockets across Mexico, and was formerly present in parts of Texas, Arizona, and New Mexico. It has been described as "scattered" in numbers and distribution. A program to release captive-bred birds has reestablished limited breeding numbers in Texas and New Mexico, and into Mexico. It still ranges through most of Central and South America as far south as Tierra del Fuego, but is absent from the forested Amazon.

Habitat: A bird of open country, the Aplomado Falcon prefers grasslands interspersed with cactus, yucca, and mesquite. It also inhabits oak and pine savannahs, areas of larger scattered trees and shrubs, and stands of trees concentrated along streams and marshes. It may also live in coastal deserts.

Behavior: Because of their ability to maneuver in tight foliage below the canopy and to chase prey on foot, Aplomado Falcons are often compared to the forest hawks (accipiters), particularly the Cooper's Hawk, which is very similar in size and habits. Aplomados also tend to perch on the inner limbs of trees and bushes, often to escape extreme heat, and are quite adept at hunting by hopping through tree branches. They often launch attacks from the tops of yuccas and other vegetation. They hunt primarily grassland birds, such as sparrows and doves; insects and even bats are also taken. The Aplomado Falcon is known to hunt well before sunrise and long after

In a male Aplomado Falcon, the supercilliary line sets off the dark crown.
—ROB PALMER

The breast of a juvenile Aplomado Falcon is streaked in dark lines. Adult females may also show narrow streaks but not as heavily. In the bird in this photo, the white upperparts are like the northern subspecies, but this photo was taken in Venezuela, so the bird must be of the South American subspecies. —ROB PALMER

sunset. It is skilled at open country tail chases and short stoops, sometimes flying into flocks of birds head-on. Watering holes are favorite hunting areas, and they have been observed exploiting prey that is fleeing grass and brush fires. One Aplomado Falcon was seen using a moving train as cover, flying alongside the train and quickly darting to the opposing side, apparently to take birds by surprise.

Aplomado Falcon pairs cooperatively hunt birds, with one individual flushing and the other attacking. Both members of a pair may feed from the same prey item simultaneously, and they sometimes remain together outside the breeding season. These pairs frequently perch side by side. Pairs will rob other raptors of their food (a behavior known as kleptoparasitism); they have also been observed stealing from herons and kingfishers. Caching uneaten or partially eaten birds is very common. These cache sites may be defended aggressively, even when devoid of food. The bird will also harass and mob people who approach too close to a food cache.

Flight: Aplomado Falcons hold their wings flat with the tips slightly upturned when gliding or soaring. They may hover above prey hiding in the brush below. When pursuing birds, their wing beats are quick and shallow in a direct flight. The wings are long and narrow with rounded tips; the tail is long and also rounded. The trailing edge of the wing has a light edge. Aplomado Falcons will readily soar, sometimes to great heights.

Breeding: The nesting season may begin as early as February. Breeding pairs take over old stick nests of other raptors, such as White-tailed Kites and Harris's Hawks. Chihuahuan Raven nests are plentiful and are also used. Nests are usually low (under 20 feet, or 6 meters, high) and may be in bushes, yucca, or mesquite. Eggs may also be laid in natural depressions in the tops of yuccas, in the pockets formed between palm trees and fronds, and occasionally on the ground in natural bowls of grass clumps. Some nesting on human-made structures (such as utility poles) has been documented. In areas where Aplomado Falcons have been reintroduced, nesting has also occurred on artificial platforms and in specially designed nest boxes (with solid tops and bottoms with vertical bars in between) placed on poles and in yuccas. Typically, 2 to 3 eggs are laid, and these hatch at day 31 or 32. The young fledge at 35 days, and parents may attend to the youngsters for up to 2 months.

Vocalizations: The Aplomado Falcon has four basic calls, with the male's voice having a higher pitch than the female's. The typical falcon *kak-kak-kak* (or *kek-kek-kek*) is used near the nest site and when the bird is disturbed. The *chip* call (single or in a short series) is used in courtship, during food transfers and feeding, and when birds are hunting and defending as a pair. The wail, or warble, is used mostly by the female at the nest or cache site, and chittering is done by birds of all ages.

Movement: The Aplomado Falcon is generally a sedentary and year-round resident. In mountainous areas it may move to lower elevations in winter. Individuals may also disperse in any direction or season.

Aplomado Falcons frequently prey on abundant insects like grasshoppers. —ROB PALMER

This incoming Aplomado Falcon may be defending the nest area against intruders or defending a cache site. —ROB PALMER

Conservation: The Northern Aplomado Falcon is considered an endangered species, and would require a healthy environment to return to pre-1930s numbers. Ideal habitat is free of organochloride pesticides and protected from overgrazing and deforestation. Preserving desert, grassland, and riparian areas from degradation and development would help protect a myriad of species in addition to the Aplomado. The Aplomado Falcon is especially at risk for secondary lead poisoning from ingesting lead shot because it feeds on dove and occasionally quail, favorite quarry for human bird hunters. A solution would be to use steel or other nonlead shot, as is required in many areas. During the reintroduction program several Aplomados have been found drowned in stock water tanks in Mexico. As a solution, at least thirty "escape ramps" have been installed in the tanks to allow birds that mistakenly land in these deep water containers to scramble up to safety.

Other threats are predation by coyotes and raccoons, but these threats are minor and do not affect the species on a population level. Great Horned Owls seem to be their most important natural predator.

Subspecies in North America: The Aplomado Falcon is found only in the Americas; three subspecies are recognized, with just one in North America:

> *F. f septentrionalis:* The Northern Aplomado subspecies occurs in the United States and Mexico, and may wander south to Nicaragua and Guatemala. This is a large bird with a complete belly band and upperparts cast in gray, especially the crown; cheeks and throat are creamy.

Etymology: The species name *femoralis* means "referring to the thighs" and points to the rufous brown feathers on the legs. *Aplomado* is Spanish for "lead-colored," an apt name for this bird.

Tidbit: The Northern Aplomado Falcon was fairly common in the Southwestern United States at the beginning of the twentieth century, according to records of egg collecting, a popular hobby and business at the time. But by the 1930s it was nearly gone from the region, with the last pair breeding in New Mexico in 1952. The subspecies was listed as federally endangered in 1986. Its extirpation was almost certainly caused by humans, and may have been the result of overgrazing and the mass conversion of native grasslands to agriculture. Cattle grazing spread mesquite seeds through the native prairie grassland, converting much of it to mesquite scrubland unsuitable for Aplomado nesting. The precipitous population decline occurred before the widespread use of pesticides, but their use may have contributed to the problem later on.

In the 1980s the Santa Cruz Predatory Bird Research Group began breeding Northern Aplomado Falcons in captivity in cooperation with the Chihuahuan Desert Research Institute and the Peregrine Fund. Between 1985 and 1989 they released twenty-four fledgling Aplomados in a pilot reintroduction program in the southern Rio Grande Valley of Texas. In the 1990s the Peregrine Fund expanded the captive breeding and reintroduction program and eventually conducted releases in West Texas and New Mexico. Various federal and state agencies, private organizations,

Aplomado habitat in Texas. —ROB PALMER

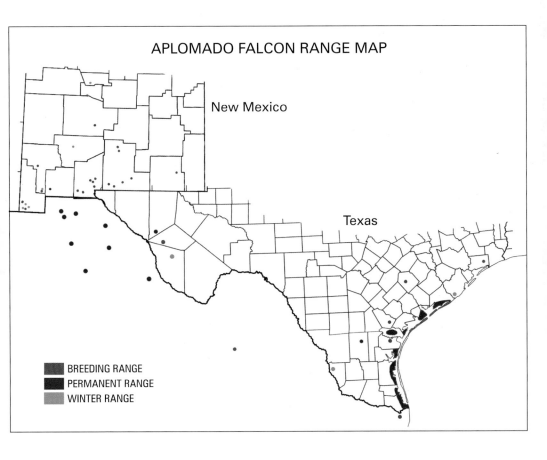

APLOMADO FALCON RANGE MAP

New Mexico

Texas

BREEDING RANGE
PERMANENT RANGE
WINTER RANGE

and individuals joined forces for this common cause. The first pair began breeding on their own in the wild in 1995 near Brownsville, Texas, with over fifty breeding pairs in southern Texas by 2007. With subsequent programs in western Texas, New Mexico, and Mexico, over 1,400 captive-bred birds have been released as of 2007, and at least fifty-six young fledged naturally from wild nests in South Texas in 2006.

Now that Aplomado Falcons have been breeding in the wild for two generations, an interesting study has documented breeding success rates. Researchers have observed that young falcons raised by wild adults have a higher survival rate than falcons that are hacked out. This has been called a higher "intrinsic fitness," with wild birds protecting their young and guiding them as they grow. It also reflects a higher recruitment rate and will certainly help the population to recover.

Private ranches have been enlisted in the Safe Harbor Program, with over 1.8 million acres in south and west Texas, and recently in southern New Mexico. Aplomado Falcons have also been listed as "nonessential experimental populations" through the Endangered Species Act. Both of these policies protect the landowners and managers from strict government regulations, creating a more cooperative arrangement with falcon researchers. Local support has been very strong, and the goal is to have another bird delisted in the near future, as the Peregrine Falcon was in 1999.

Note the seven thin white bands on the tail and the light trailing edge of the wings where they meet the body of this Aplomado Falcon. —ROB PALMER

Prairie Falcon
Falco mexicanus

Length: *male:* 14 to 16 inches (37 to 40 cm); *female:* 16 to 18 inches (42 to 47 cm)

Wingspan: *male:* 35 to 39 inches (90 to 98 cm); *female:* 40 to 45 inches (102 to 114 cm)

Weight: *male:* 14.8 to 24.1 ounces (420 to 685 grams); *female:* 23.8 to 42.7 ounces (675 to 1,210 grams)

Description: The Prairie Falcon is a large, pale brown falcon of arid, open country and is about the same size as a Peregrine Falcon. The distinguishing field trait is a triangular black patch on the underwing, or axillary region, like a dark armpit or "wing pit." It has a large squarish head with a white eyebrow, or supercilliary line that wraps around the back of the head, or nearly so, isolating a brown crown on the top of the head. It has the typical falcon dark malar stripe, sometimes called a mustache, with a white area between the eye and a darker ear patch. The Prairie Falcon has huge, dark eyes, the largest of any falcon in proportion to the head. The wingtips extend somewhat short of the tip of the tail on a perched bird. The light-colored tail contrasts with the darker upperparts, unlike the Peregrine Falcon. The sexes are very similar in plumage. Young birds have a reddish tint to the plumage and are more heavily streaked than adults. The bluish skin around the eyes, beak, and feet of juveniles turns yellow by the spring of their second year, and the streaks on the ventral plumage are mostly replaced by spots.

Range: This falcon is entirely a resident of western North America, ranging from southern Canada and the Great Plains west to the Pacific Coast, and into northern Mexico down the length of the Baja Peninsula.

Habitat: The Prairie Falcon is aptly named, inhabiting dry prairies, deserts, and open countryside with some rocky topography for nesting and hunting. It prefers grasslands and farmland, and avoids urban areas.

Behavior: This falcon uses many hunting strategies, reflecting the very different prey types it targets according to the season. Prairie Falcons that nest each spring in the Snake River Birds of Prey National Conservation Area in Idaho begin the season feeding mainly on the abundant Townsend's (Piute) Ground Squirrels that are emerging after six months underground. These squirrels reach the peak of their seasonal population numbers just as the young Prairie Falcons are beginning to fledge. In late June and July, the Townsend's Ground Squirrels retreat back into their burrows to estivate, escaping the heat and summer dryness by spending the summer in a state of torpor similar to hibernation. At this point Prairie Falcons move to another summer ground—with some flying as far as Saskatchewan and the Dakotas—and

Note the thin malar stripe and white supercilliary line, cheeks, and throat of an immature Prairie Falcon. The cere hasn't turned the bright yellow or orange of an adult. —ROB PALMER

An adult Prairie Falcon watches for intruders at the nest cliff. —ROB PALMER

A Prairie Falcon, an open country raptor that specializes in ground squirrels most of the year, hunts from a power pole. It switches to a bird diet over the winter. —ROB PALMER

switch to a different species of ground squirrel, the plentiful Richardson's. Over the winter the falcon's diet consists almost entirely of birds; then they use yet another hunting strategy, specializing in eating flocking, open country birds such as Horned Larks, buntings, and meadowlarks that they catch on or near the ground.

The Prairie Falcon cruises at moderate heights to surprise prey with low-angle attacks. Occasionally it stoops from greater heights or a cliff. It tends to glide more than soar, with wingtips pulled back slightly. It may catch swifts and swallows by flying straight through a flock in front of a cliff. Insects and lizards are eaten on occasion. Hans Peeters describes adult females killing California Jackrabbits four or five times their weight through repeated, short, swooping attacks and blows with the feet. The Prairie Falcon has been known to steal food from Northern Harriers. It also has a reputation for being exceptionally unpredictable and even cranky, and may attack other birds, especially large ones like Great Blue Herons, for no apparent reason. A Bald Eagle in Montana flew too close to a Prairie Falcon eyrie. To the astonishment of a nearby boatload of sightseers, the eagle was struck in the head; it was dead when it hit the lake. Also in Montana, a Prairie Falcon exploited large numbers of Northern Pocket Gophers that had been displaced from their burrows during a sudden river flood. She repeatedly caught the swimming rodents and returned to a power pole, eating just the front halves and dropping the remains.

Flight: Distinguishing a Prairie Falcon from a Peregrine Falcon by wing beat alone is difficult but not impossible. Dunne and Sibley describe the Prairie Falcon flight as "stiff and mechanical," as opposed to the Peregrine's "fluid, undulating ripple of movement" throughout the length of the wing. In other words, the Prairie Falcon uses a quick flick of the wrist area in flight, with the wings barely raised above the horizontal plane of the body.

Breeding: Prairie Falcons separate after the breeding season; pair bonds are established or reestablished at the breeding grounds the following year, usually in late February and March. Courtship can last for more than a month. They may be especially aggressive around the nest, even hitting people who get too close. During the breeding season, pairs have large undefended hunting territories ranging up to 15 miles (24 km) from the nest. They tolerate other Prairie Falcons, and their nests may be as close as 100 yards (90 meters) in Idaho and 300 yards (270 meters) in Wyoming. Several Peregrine Falcon and Prairie Falcon nests have been 100 yards (90 meters) apart in Montana. Close nests are not that uncommon; this is especially true when eyries of the two species are out of the line of sight from each other.

Prairie Falcons often nest on cliffs, either in a deep hole or recess in the rock, or in a scrape on a ledge; they may take over a stick nest of a hawk or raven built on a cliff. A rocky bluff, isolated rocky outcrop, riverbank, or even a tree may also be used. Prairie Falcons have benefited from artificial ledges and potholes dug into cliffs, both created by humans for that purpose. Nests are usually in the upper half of the cliff face, and are nearly always located under an overhang or other feature that will minimize the threat of extreme temperatures. Eggs number 3 to 5, rarely 6, and the female does all of the nighttime and most of the daytime incubation and brooding

At least four Prairie Falcon nests are on these cliffs in Northern Colorado, mostly in cracks and potholes. —KATE DAVIS

The dark axillaries are the telltale field marks of a Prairie Falcon. —ROB PALMER

.Prairie Falcon chicks on a nest ledge that has been used for generations. You can see the whitewash for some distance. —ROB PALMER

of young. The young fledge at 36 to 41 days; the parent female then moves on to her summer grounds. Like some other species of raptors (such as Ferruginous Hawks), the male stays longer to feed the fledglings. Young disperse at around 65 days. The young females remain on their natal territories longer than males.

In 1905 artist and naturalist Louis Agassiz Fuertes described a Prairie Falcon nest on an island in Pyramid Lake, Nevada. It lay on a 400-foot (120-meter) cliff in the center of a colony of nesting pelicans. He wrote of quail and jay feathers strewn around the base of the cliff—prey birds that the Prairie Falcon pair must have carried from land 1.5 miles (2.4 km) away.

Vocalizations: Prairie Falcons makes sounds similar to those made by the Gyrfalcon, and some experts say Prairie Falcon calls may be undistinguishable from those of Peregrines. Both sexes make the standard, large falcon *echup* call at breeding, the chitter when faced with danger, and the *kik-kik-kik* call when they spot intruders or when they are excited. The male *kaks* may be higher in pitch than those of females. The female may whine for food.

Movement: Some Prairie Falcons have distinct breeding, summer, and wintering grounds and engage in loop migration. In midsummer these three-tier migrants move from their breeding grounds in search of better hunting opportunities. They move on to their wintering grounds in autumn, mostly in the Great Plains and south to Texas, to feed largely on birds. Prairie Falcons often show a high degree of fidelity at all three seasonal territories, not just the breeding grounds, returning to the same areas the following year.

During migration the Prairie Falcon relies less on ridge thermals and winds than other raptors do. Like Peregrine Falcons, their spring trip back to the breeding ground takes less time than the fall migration. Perhaps they move with a single purpose in mind. Prairie Falcons in the southwestern United States and northern Mexico tend to be more sedentary and may move only in altitude, seeking higher ground after breeding.

Conservation: Prairie Falcon populations can be negatively impacted by nearby disturbances, including mining and oil and gas development. In Central California, only one breeding territory out of thirty-three was still occupied after the native grasslands were converted to agriculture. Prairie Falcons are a species of concern in the United States and considered threatened in Mexico, while populations are considered stable in Canada.

Subspecies in North America: The Prairie Falcon is monotypic, with just one species occurring worldwide. There are different color phases, with certain geographic ranges having particularly dark or light plumages. Interestingly, the Prairie Falcon and Peregrine Falcon have been known to hybridize in the wild, but it is extremely rare.

Etymology: The species name *mexicanus* describes the first place that a specimen was collected, Mexico.

Two young Prairie Falcons await a food delivery at an eyrie in Wyoming. The ventral streaks will be replaced with spots in adulthood. A third chick had left the nest on foot and was 20 yards (18 meters) away on the cliff. —ROB PALMER

A Prairie Falcon rockets across the front of the nest cliff. They can be especially intolerant of intruders, even those that pose no threat, like herons and vultures. —ROB PALMER

Tidbit: A great deal of research has been conducted in the Snake River Birds of Prey National Conservation Area in Idaho, a hotbed of activity for Prairie Falcons and other raptors. This rough and wild refuge is 600,000 acres of public land established by Congress in 1993 and administered by the Bureau of Land Management. It has the highest densities of breeding raptors in the world, with six hundred nesting pairs of fifteen different species. Prairie Falcons are the most numerous, nesting on virtually every suitable cliff, sometimes with two nests on the same tall face with one above the other. They tolerate other falcons and avoid aggressive interactions by flying high over the cliffs to head to the hunting grounds.

Recent wildfires in the region have dramatically altered the native vegetation, causing fluctuations in Townsend's Ground Squirrel populations. Native plants still exist in undisturbed areas, but nonnative vegetation has taken over burned sites. Other factors that affect squirrel numbers and Prairie Falcon breeding success have been drought, livestock grazing, and agricultural development. A little-understood issue has been military training conducted on the conservation area, which may disturb foraging falcons or cause slight alterations in the habitat.

A Prairie Falcon hunts game low over the ground,
seeking a surprise ambush. —ROB PALMER

Male Prairie Falcons are often found on fence posts, whereas the females tend to perch higher on utility poles when both poles and fences are present. —ROB PALMER

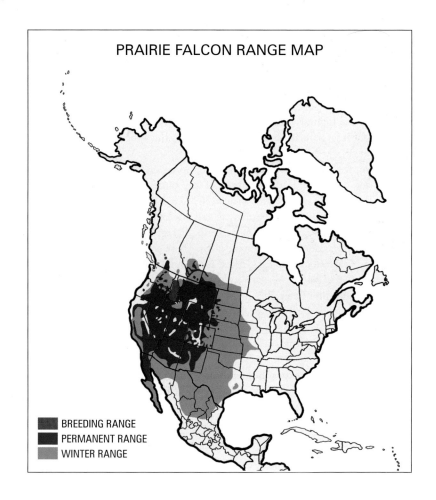

PRAIRIE FALCON RANGE MAP

BREEDING RANGE
PERMANENT RANGE
WINTER RANGE

Peregrine Falcon
Falco peregrinus

Length: *male:* 14.2 to 19.3 inches (36 to 49 cm); *female:* 17.7 to 22.8 inches (45 to 58 cm)

Wingspan: *male:* 37 inches (94 cm); *female:* 40 inches (102 cm)

Weight: *male:* 18.6 to 37.3 ounces (528 to 1,058 grams); *female:* 28.1 to 56.2 ounces (797 to 1,595 grams)

Description: The Peregrine Falcon, which may be the most studied bird in the world, is famous for its cosmopolitan distribution and its story as a survivor of environmental contaminants. The North American varieties are medium to large falcons, about the same size as the Prairie Falcon (male as large as a crow, female raven sized). In contrast to the Prairie Falcon, the Peregrine's underwings in flight seem uniformly dark. The adult is slate gray to bluish to nearly black above, barred below, with a light or white chest and throat. Its head is marked with a dark "helmet" and large malar stripes, even in juvenal plumage. When perched, its wing tips extend to or nearly to the end of the relatively short tail. The female is noticeably larger than the male. Young birds have a slightly longer tail than adults and are brown above and heavily streaked below until their first molt during their second summer. Juvenal skin color changes from bluish to yellow and sometimes orange, except for some western Continental (*F. p. anatum*) birds that have yellow legs at fledging. This coloration appears to be related to diet. Some brown juvenal feathers may persist for a few years. The Peregrine has the highest wing loading of all of the falcons, meaning that its body mass or weight is large relative to the surface area of the wings.

Range: Along with Barn Owls, Ospreys, and Common Ravens, Peregrine Falcons are among the mostly widest distributed of any birds in the world. They inhabit the widest latitudinal range of any bird species (78° N to 56° S), from north of the Arctic Circle to the tip of South America, and are found on every continent except Antarctica. As they follow migrating seabirds, Peregrines even visit the Hawaiian Islands, the most remote island chain on earth. There are no breeding populations in Iceland, New Zealand, or tropical Central and South America.

Habitat: Although the Peregrine inhabits a wide range of habitats from desert to moist coastal areas, they tend to prefer open country, relying on wide expanses for hunting. Once dependent on rock cliffs for breeding, they now regularly nest on tall buildings, bridges, and power plant stacks in urban areas.

Behavior: Peregrines are expert hunters, with birds constituting an estimated 77 to 99 percent of their diet. They prey on more then three hundred species of birds in the Northern Hemisphere, from passerines (perching birds) to small geese. The most numerous prey items worldwide are pigeons and doves (Columbidae); Peregrines

This adult female Peregrine is of the Continental subspecies. Dick Dekker describes the Peregrine's dark eyes and gaze as "magnanimous, docile, free of menace."
—KATE DAVIS

After this Peregrine lands and is still, its cryptic coloration will blend into the rock surroundings, making it surprisingly difficult to spot. —ROB PALMER

The wide malar stripe of an adult Peregrine forms a dark helmet that contrasts with the yellow eye ring and cere. —ROB PALMER

exploited the billions of Passenger Pigeons before that species became extinct in the early 1900s. Peregrine Falcons will specialize in whatever species is locally common, and some individuals are connoisseurs who eat one or two species exclusively. Most prey is captured in the air. Some coastal Peregrines may strike their prey over water, braking to "helicopter down" to retrieve the carcass and carry it ashore. Peregrines also eat small mammals, including bats, especially at dusk and dawn as the bats emerge from or retreat to their roosting caves.

Insects are sometimes "hawked" (caught) in the air, and Peregrines have been seen catching dozens of salmonflies with their feet and transferring them to their mouths in flight. One female caught twenty-three salmonflies in just a few minutes with no misses! Nesting Peregrines in Arizona, especially females on guard duty near the nest, were observed capturing large numbers of cicadas. Not widely reported in the literature, feeding on insects may be more common than previously thought.

Peregrine have also been known to steal food from other birds. Joel Pagel describes a nest in which the falcon pair routinely robbed Ospreys of fish, and he reports finding the remains of steelhead in some nests. Other Peregrines have been observed stealing mammalian prey from hawks; some Peregrines also eat carrion.

Using height for observation and stealth, and combining gravity with flying skills, Peregrines are best known for the classic power stoop, a close-winged dive begun from 500 to 2,000 feet (150 to 600 meters) above the ground. The stoop may be completely vertical, or relatively shallow at 30 to 45 degrees to the horizontal. Speeds of 200 mph (320 km/h) or more (perhaps 230 mph or 370 km/h) can be reached in a long, steep dive. In level flight, Peregrines occasionally reach 60 mph (97 km/h), and normal traveling flight averages around 30 mph (48 km/h).

Using their feet for hunting, Peregrines may hit a prey bird in the head, back, or wing. They may fly past a bird on the wing and rip it open with the talon of the hallux (back toe). The falcon may ambush birds from below, flipping over in flight to attack the soft feathers of the prey bird's belly. They will "bind to" smaller prey and drag the birds along, or grab larger birds and ride them to the ground for the coup de grâce. The Peregrine may strike and injure prey in the air, catching the animal before it hits the ground, or eat the animal where it falls. Prey will dodge and try to head for cover, or fly higher to escape in "ringing up" flight. Ducks may be reluctant to leave the water with a Peregrine in the air, or may retreat underwater and stay there as long as possible, resurfacing in the protection of emergent vegetation. A mated pair of Peregrines may hunt in tandem from courtship through fledging of young.

Michael Henon observed bat-hunting Peregrines on the west coast of Mexico during the winters of 2002 to 2006. These birds benefit from the oceanfront hotels and streetlights from which they fly to hunt, often long after dark. The Peregrines arrived about five minutes before the bats emerged to fly inland. They attacked from behind to avoid being detected by the bats through echolocation; attacks from the sides were always unsuccessful. Up to three adult falcons could be observed at once, with small defended hunting territories, "seemingly hopscotching down the coast using hotels as stopovers."

Flight: The Peregrine Falcon has a strong but rather shallow wing beat that has been described as fluid. The outer half of the wing is long and pointed, but can be changed

These cliffs at Blackleaf Canyon on the Rocky Mountain Front near Choteau, Montana, have been home to a pair of Peregrines since 2006. Volunteers from the Montana Peregrine Institute monitoring the birds observe a food exchange. —KATE DAVIS

Not Photoshopped! An adult Peregrine Falcon attacks a Brown Pelican. —WILL SOOTER

to a more rounded shape when soaring. The wings are held flat when gliding; the tail is tapered with a square tip. When the wings and tail are spread, the Peregrine may be mistaken for a hawk or raven from a distance.

Breeding: Courtship displays of the Peregrine Falcon are spectacular. The male often performs stoops and dives in front of the nest cliff, rolling from side to side to show off the flash of an alternating light front and dark back. The male brings his mate prey items in food exchanges that often occur in midair and with great dexterity. The exchange may be foot to foot with the female flipping upside down, or the male may drop the prey for her to catch. Writes biologist Joseph Hagar of the breathtaking courtship flights, "The sheer excitement of watching such a performance was tremendous; we felt a strong impulse to stand and cheer." Exchanges also take place when the female is perched.

Peregrines rely on vertical property—cliffs, cut banks, and, recently, the sides of tall buildings—for nesting. In a paper in 1942, Joseph J. Hickey classified three types of nesting cliffs. First-class cliffs are "extremely high, often rather long, usually overlooking water, and generally dominating the surrounding countryside." These cliffs would attract birds year after year despite the shootings and raids by oologists (egg collectors) that were common at the time. Second-class cliffs are smaller and can withstand human interference, but to a lesser degree, and may be abandoned for periods of time. Third-class cliffs are not very high and may or may not overlook water. One in Montana was on a 50-foot (15-meter) dirt embankment. These are the "marginal niches in Peregrine ecology" and may be occupied when sites of the first two types are already taken by other breeders. A fourth type was proposed by Richard Bond. These are small islands, even without cliffs, important to the Northwest Coastal Peale's subspecies. The Continental subspecies nests on islands in the Baja region where there are no terrestrial predators.

Breeding cliffs range from river cut banks to sheer rock walls over a 1,000 feet (300 meters) in height. Typically a horizontal ledge is chosen, with an overhang above to keep the nest out of the elements; shrubs or other vegetation sometimes hides the nestling falcons, much to the dismay of researchers. A crack or pothole in a cliff is occasionally used. It is not uncommon for a nesting pair of Peregrines to take over the abandoned stick nest of a raven, hawk, or Golden Eagle. Curiously, a tree-nesting population in Tennessee existed and Peregrines were reported to nest in cavities in sycamore trees in Kansas and Illinois in the late 1800s. Currently some birds in the Pacific Northwest near Arcata, California, are nesting in redwood trees.

Breeding pairs usually return to the same area every year, but often switch nest ledges on the same cliff or alternate cliffs in successive years. Some individuals will use a preferred ledge or pothole for their entire reproductive life. The average age for both sexes to breed is two years. Males sometimes don't start breeding until age three or older. Yearlings have bred successfully; this is more common for females. Usually 3 to 4 eggs are laid, with rare instances of 6 eggs reported. The eggs are laid just over 48 hours apart. Incubation of each egg lasts for 32 to 35 days, and usually begins with the laying of the penultimate (next to last) egg. Birds nesting at higher elevations might begin incubation with the first egg. Some females will wait until

A Peregrine in flight.
—KATE DAVIS

Tufts of down are still present on the head of a brown youngster (to the right of her father). Although the flight feathers are not completely grown, she is able to fly, but not with great strength. —NICK DUNLOP

a full clutch is laid. Both sexes share daytime incubation duties; the female usually incubates at night. Chicks make their first flights at around 37 to 45 days, with the larger females usually taking longer to leave the nest than the males. Young falcons may practice hunting by dropping objects such as sticks, moss, and prey remains for their siblings to catch. For their first hunting forays they often hunt insects, and after considerable practice begin catching and eating birds. The young depend on their parents for additional food from 1 to 3 months after fledging.

Vocalizations: The *kak* of an irritated Peregrine Falcon resonates off cliffs and canyons and indicates that a nesting pair is in the area. Vocalizations are almost entirely associated with breeding. Both sexes have an *eechup* call and a high wailing call given during some close encounters between individuals, such as food exchanges. Offspring and female mates beg for food with a repeated *kree* call.

Movement: The three North American subspecies have different migration habits, from the long-distance-traveling Tundra to the largely sedentary Peale's, which apparently remains in the Aleutian Island chain throughout winter. Some Peale's Peregrines from the coast and islands adjacent to mainland Alaska and British Columbia migrate down the coast in the fall, occasionally as far south as Baja California, Mexico, but generally no further than the north-central California coast.

All of the northernmost Continental Peregrines migrate south, but birds from southern Canada on south usually move short distances or not at all. Movement is also dependant on altitude. Peregrines at lower elevations may remain on the breeding ground year-round. Seasonal abandonment of nest sites is as brief as possible, often brought about by inclement weather. Birds at higher elevations will move into lower valleys and down to the coast during bad weather.

The Arctic Tundra Peregrine migrates the farthest, from its far northern breeding grounds to wintering grounds in Central and South America, a distance of 7,000 to 8,000 miles (11,300 to 12,900 km). Some birds fly as far south as central Argentina and Chile. A study by the Southern Cross Peregrine Project found that some individual birds migrated near sea level, while other birds flew at up to 16,000 feet (4,900 meters) through the Andes. One bird marked in Chile had a route of 9,402 miles (15,131 km), ending up north of the arctic circle. Peregrines tend to exhibit leapfrog migration, with the birds that nest the farthest north flying the farthest south. Arctic Tundra Peregrines often pool up on the Texas coast near Padre Island, a major staging area for many migratory birds.

Conservation: Peregrine Falcons' status has changed dramatically over the course of fifty years. Estimates before World War II for North America are that there were 7,000 to 10,000 breeding pairs. However, thorough surveys were difficult to carry out at the time, so the accuracy of this number is impossible to know. By the early 1970s, when DDT was banned and they were added to the endangered species list, Peregrines had been extirpated in the East and nearly so in the western United States. Recovery efforts have been successful, and currently many states have more Peregrines than ever before. The estimated Continental Falcon population at the end of the twentieth century was 8,000 to 10,000 pairs and increasing. By counting

A young Peregrine Falcon chases a Turkey Vulture, probably just in play—a safe way to hone their flight skills. The photographer notes that all of the young he observes in California love to chase vultures. —NICK DUNLOP

With its cosmopolitan range and impressive habits, the Peregrine Falcon is probably the most studied bird in the world . —NICK DUNLOP

the nonbreeders (immatures and floaters) these numbers could be as high as 50,000 individuals. They were taken off the endangered species list in 1999. Time will tell if they will be more common than in pre-DDT times when their population levels stabilize. Recent migration counts in the Northeast show the numbers to be leveling off after a long period of growth.

Subspecies in North America: Nineteen subspecies are recognized worldwide. Birds in the Midwest and eastern U.S. are reintroduced and are hybrids of up to seven subspecies. They are called "Eastern Peregrines." For a majority, the background color on their underside is basically white (rather than having the salmon cast of *F. p. anatum*) with barring on the breast. In addition to the hybrid "Eastern Peregrine," three subspecies are found in North America.

> *F. p. anatum:* The Continental or American Peregrine subspecies. It breeds in the western United States and the forests, or taiga, of Canada and Alaska. It has a clearly defined malar stripe; the white of the chest and belly often has a pinkish, rufous, or salmon cast. Some individuals in Alberta have a white overall color on their underside, like the other two subspecies.

> *F. p. tundrius:* The Tundra or, as it is sometimes called, the Arctic Peregrine. Clayton White felt that "the distinctively marked tundra breeding population of Peregrines merited formal scientific recognition," and so first classified *F. p. tundrius* in 1968. It is the smallest of the North American subspecies and is paler overall, and the barring on the belly is very fine. The malar stripe is dark and narrow, and the auricular (ear) area has extensive white with no central spotting. The crown or helmet area is less defined than that of *F. p. anatum*, and the adult doesn't have a salmon wash on the breast. Immature birds have a very light blond crown.

> *F. p. pealei:* The Peale's Peregrine is the largest subspecies worldwide. It inhabits the coastal Pacific Northwest from the Aleutian Islands north to the mainland coast of Alaska, and south along the British Columbia coast to about northwestern Washington. It is dark overall. The malar stripe is large and clearly defined. Adults, especially females, usually have extensive spotting in the auricular area and on the bib, or upper chest. Adults also have heavy barring below. An immature Peale's falcon can be mistaken for a Gyrfalcon.

Etymology: John James Audubon and other early writers called one now-extinct eastern variety the Big-footed Hawk. Another early common name was Long-footed Falcon, a description of the length of its toes. The descriptive word *peregrine* means "foreign" or "having a tendency to wander," from the Latin *peregrinus* for "foreign." This refers to the fact that some Peregrines migrate long distances. *Anatum* comes from the Latin *anas* or *anatis*, meaning "duck." Although Peregrines only occasionally prey on them, ducks were thought to be a major food source at the time of naming; the common name was formerly Duck Hawk for the same reason. The name *tundrius* refers to that subspecies' tundra habitat. And *pealei* comes from the man for whom the subspecies was named, Titian R. Peale, an early nineteenth-century artist and taxidermist from Philadelphia.

A Peregrine starts to mantle a killed Chukar to hide it from potential thieves, or kleptoparasites. —KATE DAVIS

This young Tundra Peregrine was trapped and banded on the Washington coast. —TRACY FLEMING

| *F. p. anatum* | *F. p. tundrius* | *F. p. pealei* |

Tidbit: Records tell of Peregrine Falcons nesting on human-made structures such as cathedrals and abandoned castles hundreds of years ago in Europe. Before their re-introduction in North America this was a very rare occurrence in the eastern United States, with just three nests on buildings (in Montreal, Philadelphia, and New York City) and one on an abandoned stone bridge pier. They were not reported to nest on any buildings in the west. Today Peregrines have adapted to city life and are thriving in urban settings across North America. Tall structures with narrow ledges mimic the rock cliffs of their natural habitat, and plenty of food in the form of pigeons and other birds is available. Nest sites high on buildings offer protection from their primary predators, raccoons and Great Horned Owls. City life isn't without its hazards, though. Collisions with moving cars and reflective windows are an especially difficult problem for fledgling falcons. Remarkably, collisions seem to have decreased somewhat over the years as these birds have modified their behavior to fit the new landscape.

Where the falcon has nested on buildings, humans have usually assisted by pro-viding special nest boxes lined with aquarium or pea gravel (not to mention webcams so researchers and birdwatchers can observe). By the early 1990s, the Peregrine Falcon had taken up residence in sixty U.S. cities. New York City has the most, with about fifteen resident pairs in 2003.

Today, 70 percent of Peregrines breeding in the Midwest are nesting on human-built structures. Figures from 2006 of 172 nesting pairs show that the most widely used structures are buildings, with just over half of the nest sites. Birds returned to their historic haunts on the Mississippi River in 2000 and are back to using natural cliff sites, with just under a third of the nests located there. Power plant stacks with their proximity to water and the associated avian prey base have about a fifth of the nests. Bridges are also used, especially in West Coast cities, but mortality is higher on these structures, as young may plunge into the water and drown. They are the sites for 12 percent of nesting attempts.

For city-dwelling humans, being in the proximity of nesting Pere-grines—enigmas and symbols of wil-derness and hunting prowess—must be a thrill to some. And to others, it may mean the stunning sight of hav-ing pigeon parts and entrails falling from the sky to the sidewalk, the Peregrine high above!

An urban Peregrine in San Jose, California. —EVET LOEWEN

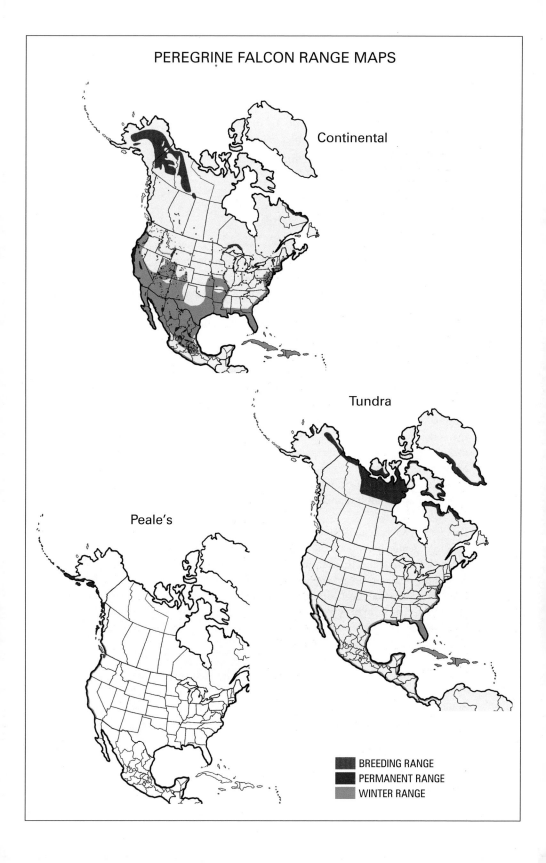

PEREGRINE FALCON RANGE MAPS

Continental

Tundra

Peale's

BREEDING RANGE
PERMANENT RANGE
WINTER RANGE

Gyrfalcon

Falco rusticolus

Length: *male:* 19 to 21 inches (50 to 54 cm); *female:* 22 to 24 inches (57 to 61 cm)

Wingspan: *male:* 43 to 47 inches (110 to 120 cm); *female:* 49 to 51 inches (124 to 130 cm)

Weight: *male:* 35.3 to 45.9 ounces (1,000 to 1,300 grams); *female:* 49.4 to 74.1 ounces (1,400 to 2,100 grams)

Description: The Gyrfalcon is the largest falcon in the world, impressive in stature, speed, and successful survival in an inhospitable landscape. Its plumage ranges from white and light gray to dark gray and black, with every gradation in between. Natural selection may favor one color or another for camouflage or other purposes. Plumage doesn't change seasonally, like the ptarmigan, their chief winter prey item. The Gyrfalcon is heavy bodied and deep chested, with wide shoulders and rather rounded wingtips for a falcon. It has a long tail that appears tapered when the bird is perched. When perched, its wingtips extend to about two-thirds the length of the tail. Its malar stripe is less distinct than that of the Peregrine and Prairie Falcon; it also lacks the "helmet" of the Peregrine. The Gyrfalcon can completely cover its feet with its long belly feathers when standing. It has softer feathers and more down for insulation than other falcons. It is most commonly observed perched on a cliff or a prominent rock, or on the ground. Birds that overwinter near civilization may be seen perching on human-made structures such as utility and fence poles, grain elevators, buildings, hay bales, and even duck hunting blinds. Juveniles are more heavily streaked than adults and attain adult plumage and skin color at two to three years of age.

Range: The Gyrfalcon is Holarctic, inhabiting the Arctic and sub-Arctic across the northern hemisphere. It is found in Canada, Alaska, Greenland, Iceland, Norway, Sweden, Finland, and Russia. Certain color variants are related to geographic location. Individuals in Greenland and the Arctic islands of Canada are usually white. Dark individuals are most common in Canada and don't occur in Eurasia. Tom Cade points out that in one region of northern Quebec, the whitest and blackest birds breed side by side with every intermediate color variant. The Gyrfalcon breeds from sea level up to 5,350 feet (1,630 meters).

Habitat: A bird of Arctic tundra and taiga, the Gyrfalcon prefers open country, often along waterways and lakes. Mountainous terrain offers nesting cliffs and vantage points for hunting. Rocky seacoasts and offshore islands where colonial seabirds nest are also prime hunting habitat. Many birds stay in the tundra year-round, while others winter near farmlands, prairies, beaches, and even airports. Individual birds have been found to return to the same wintering territory year after year.

The gray phase of the Gyrfalcon lacks the distinct malar stripe and helmet markings of the Peregrine Falcon. —ROB PALMER

A female Gyrfalcon displays a gray morph, or variant. This species is the largest falcon in the world. —KATE DAVIS

An Alaska river bottom is Gyrfalcon country. —ROB PALMER

Behavior: Gyrfalcons specialize in feeding on Rock and Willow Ptarmigans year-round in northern North America. They are also adept at catching ground squirrels, which they especially target in the spring. Ptarmigans are usually killed on the ground or as they take flight, and Gyrfalcons are capable of taking birds as large as geese. The most common method of attack is an ambush from a fast, low glide over the surrounding terrain; diving on prey from high above is less common. Gyrfalcons may also hunt from a perch or tail chase for long distances. Pairs may hunt cooperatively together to exhaust and overcome prey. Coastal Gyrfalcons specialize in hunting seabirds; father inland the falcon may hunt perching birds, such as finches, buntings, and longspurs.

In the tundra, prey species of ptarmigan, lemmings, and hares exhibit population fluctuations, and the Gyrfalcon may alter its behavior accordingly. In years when prey is scarce, the Gyrfalcon may abstain from breeding, which often results in a mass winter migration. During years of these irruptive movements, the contiguous United States may have large numbers of Gyrfalcons; other northern birds, such as Goshawks and Snowy and Great Gray Owls, may be seen as well.

Flight: The Gyrfalcon has deep, powerful wing beats that may appear rather slow. Its fast, long, sustained flight allows it to chase down and overcome waterfowl. It may fly at night more than other falcons.

Breeding: Gyrfalcons often take over the abandoned stick nests of other cliff-breeding birds, such as the Golden Eagle, Rough-legged Hawk, or Common Raven; in certain areas this occurs most or nearly all of the time. They sometimes take over raven nests that are being constructed or are newly built; this does not happen with eagle nests. In some locales, the Gyrfalcon will use raven and eagle nests in trees. Scrapes on cliff ledges are also used. The eyrie can often be spotted from a distance because bright yellow-green lichens, fertilized by excrement, grow below it on the rocks. The Gyrfalcon has also nested on oil pipelines, mining structures of gold dredges, and sluice boxes. Stick nests are usually destroyed over the course of the season by the youngsters, and so are not often used in successive years.

Typically 3 to 4 eggs are laid, and these hatch at around 35 days. The young double in weight by their fifth day, and can pull apart delivered prey at 4 weeks old. They fly at 45 to 50 days old and become independent of their parents after1 month to 6 weeks, at which time they hunt passerines, rodents, and young ptarmigans.

Vocalizations: Nearly all vocalizations occur during the breeding season, and are typical of the large falcons. The *kak, kak, kak* alarm, mobbing, and male courtship calls are all a little deeper and more guttural than those of the Peregrine Falcon. Both sexes may emit a *chup* when perched, during courtship, and in food transfers. The female gives a *skree* call when begging for food.

Movement: Some birds, usually adult males, are year-round residents at their tundra breeding grounds. These individuals may exhibit nesting behavior as early as January. First-year birds tend to migrate farther south and, along with adult females, make up

In the flight of a Gyrfalcon, wingbeats seem slow because they are powerful and deep.
—ROB PALMER

A Gyrfalcon eyrie in Alaska. In some regions nearly all of the falcons use stick nests built by Rough-legged Hawks, ravens, and Golden Eagles. They are rarely used two years in a row as the young usually destroy the structure. —ROB PALMER

These Gyrfalcon chicks at the nest are probably about three weeks old. They will grow quickly and leave the nest at forty-five to fifty days. —ROB PALMER

the majority of the migrants. Migrants generally stay north of 40°N latitude (northern California and Colorado, across to mid-Ohio and New Jersey). In exceptional years, Gyrfalcons will migrate to the south-central United States, with records as far south as Oklahoma and Texas.

Conservation: Because of their remote Arctic habitat, Gyrfalcons have been spared many of the misfortunes that have plagued other falcon species. Pesticide contamination is less of problem in the Arctic than in other parts of the world, and their prey is nonmigratory, reducing the chances of contaminants being brought in from elsewhere. Habitat destruction thus far has been minimized. And the scarcity of people has meant limited direct persecution through shooting and trapping. The Gyrfalcon may be particularly affected by climate change, and will be closely watched.

Subspecies in North America: Color variants were once considered as separate subspecies and at one point forty were described. Now the Gyrfalcon is recognized as monotypic, unusual for a bird with such a large geographical distribution.

Etymology: These birds have been called Gyr Falcon, Jerfalcon, Gerfalcon, Greenland Falcon, and Iceland Falcon. There are many theories as to the origin of *gyr*. It may come from the old German *gir* for "vulture," from a root word meaning "greed"; this could reflect the Gyrfalcon's large size or seemingly gluttonous habits. Or it may derive from the Greek *hiero-*, meaning "sacred," referring to their lofty place in the medieval world of falconry as the bird reserved for the king alone. The species name, *rusticolus*, means "living in the country," or Arctic tundra in this case.

Tidbit: The Gyrfalcon is a member of the subgenus *Hierofalco*, which includes the closely related Saker, Lanner, and Lagger Falcons. This is based on morphology, behavior, habitat, and DNA studies. Recent genetic studies have shown the Gyrfalcon to be truly monotypic, but with two separate and distinct populations. One is in Greenland and Iceland; a second, separate population inhabits Alaska, Canada, Russia, and Norway in a gene flow across from Russia. The study suggests that one recent ancestor gave rise to the circumpolar Gyrfalcon during a rapid expansion in Pleistocene time.

A Gyrfalcon scraps with two ravens. Falcons have a real sense of play and may engage in harmless aerobatics with other birds. —ROB PALMER

A young white phase Gyrfalcon in training for falconry. The largest and fastest of the falcon species, Gyrfalcons are prized for the sport. —ROB PALMER

GYRFALCON RANGE MAP

BREEDING RANGE
PERMANENT RANGE
WINTER RANGE
- - - WINTER DISPERSAL

Four Continental Peregrine fledglings, all female. —NICK DUNLOP

Appendix 1

PROTOCOLS FOR FALCON NEST OBSERVATIONS

These guidelines are for professional field researchers; while some of these protocols are not directly applicable to amateur birders and photographers, they provide useful information on observing falcons and maintaining the safety of both birds and observers. At no time should anyone other than a professional researcher attempt to enter a nest or handle young birds.

Observing falcons in the field can be both the most exciting and the most painfully tedious work a researcher or land manager can engage in. Happening upon a falcon hunting is often pure luck, and the amount of observation time involving something exciting, such as a kill, might be over in the blink of an eye. More often than not the falcon is perched on a pole, tree, or cliff for the duration of the observation visit. At migration sites throughout North America, raptors may be overwhelming in numbers and activity, or there may be nothing for hours and even days. Protocols for observation are established to ensure special care is taken at nests, where careless actions by humans may mean life or death to falcon offspring. Observers have the challenge of obtaining rigorous data to help in the protection of the species, and provide information for raptorphiles of the future.

Above all, the well-being of the birds takes precedence over any data collected, observations made, or photographs taken. Nest disturbances must always be avoided or minimized; this is especially critical for nest entries or handling of young or adults, and these activities are tightly regulated by the U.S. Fish and Wildlife Service and state agencies. Richard Fyfe and Richard "Butch" Olendorff addressed the issue of protecting raptors from human activities *and* biologists in their 1976 paper "Minimizing the Dangers of Nesting Studies to Raptors and Other Sensitive Species." Joel Pagel followed in this vein with cliff-specific guidelines in a 1991 paper titled "Protocol for Observing Known and Potential Peregrine Falcon Eyries in the Pacific Northwest." Using these two publications, researchers can establish a methodology for obtaining practical and defensible data in a manner that is safe for the observer and the birds. The casual birdwatcher, hobbyist photographer, and professional researcher alike will benefit from the suggestions in publications. Fyfe and Olendorff's guidance continues to inform the actions of raptor biologists with the following credo: "Knowledgeable trespass on a bird's territory—or none at all." Some consider their paper a "must-read" prior to any raptor nest work.

Fyfe and Olendorff address the biological and ecological detriments of biologists' presence associated with nest observation and place their concerns into the following categories.

1. Desertion

After an encounter with humans, raptors engaged in reproductive attempts may leave the eggs or young and not return. Certain species and some individual pairs may be more likely to desert. American Kestrels, for example, tend to be more tolerant, whereas some cliff nesters abandon their selected ledge, especially when there is human activity above or next to the nest. After a blind was installed near a Gyrfalcon nest, the male disappeared; the young survived thanks to the diligent female. Desertion is less likely to occur later in the breeding cycle, after the parent birds have put more energy into the nesting process. However, even when chicks are large, some individual adults may not come back for hours or even longer. During a storm or on an open, exposed, or unshaded ledge, this could mean death for the young.

2. Damage to Eggs and Young by Frightened Adults

Adults can puncture or crush eggs, or trample the young in a frantic exit from the nest. Falcons often place their feet beneath and between eggs and hatchlings when brooding. The eggs or young may be catapulted from the ledge or stick nest by an adult's hasty exit. Instead of sneaking up on a nest, biologists should ensure the parent birds are aware of their approach and have time to depart safely. When making nest entries during incubating or brooding, researchers should make their presence known by talking, singing, and lightly clapping as an audible warning to the attending birds.

A male Peregrine repeatedly landed on the grassy ledge to the left, claiming it as occupied.
—KATE DAVIS

3. Cooling, Overheating, and Loss of Moisture from Eggs

Embryo death can result if the eggs get too cool or too hot. Exposure to direct sunlight is especially deadly, even for short durations. Mortality occurs if the egg temperature rises above the embryo body temperature (105 degrees Fahrenheit, or 41 degrees Celsius). Dehydration may be dangerous at hatching time if eggs are left without the transfer of moisture from a brooding parent; high humidity has been shown to be critical for eggs that are artificially incubated. Nest visits by researchers must be short, and eggs can be placed in a glove or covered from the sun. Researchers and observers should avoid nest visits whenever possible during incubation, hatch, and immediately post-hatch; obviously, nest entries should not be conducted at the hottest time of the day.

4. Chill and Heat Prostration of Nestlings

Growing chicks cannot thermoregulate, or maintain their own body temp-erature, so parents must keep them from getting too cold or too warm. Nestlings are safe during brief visits at temperatures to about 45 degrees Fahrenheit (7 degrees Celsius), but below this require warmth. Falcon young, as well as eggs, can withstand cooling better than overheating. Heat can be deadly, so cliff-nesting raptor parents provide shade with outstretched wings or their shadow when necessary, at least for the first two and a half weeks after the chicks are born. By this age the young can pant or retreat to the shade to keep cool. Prairie Falcons chicks appear to handle the heat better than other cliff-nesting falcon chicks.

This Prairie Falcon nest was photographed in the 1960s. —RON AUSTING

5. Missed Feedings

Nutrition and hydration are extremely important to the growing bodies and feathers of falcon chicks; very young falcons can die from missed feedings. Fyfe and Olendorff stress that a "naturalist must appreciate the burdens [he] places on the animals [he] studies and be willing to compensate for them."

6. Premature Fledging

More than any other raptors, falcons are likely to prematurely fledge during nest entries or in the presence of a potential predator. Fledging behavior is age- and sex-dependent. At the appearance of a predator (humans included), young birds typically sit motionless, back away from the source of danger, or quickly move to the other side of the nest. The researcher can block their escape by putting a leg over the nest opening. If the researcher suspects the chick is about to prematurely fledge (bolt), the nest should not be entered (unless it is low in height above the ground). Special care must be given if the nest is over or near water, and an assistant should remain below in a boat to quickly rescue a bird if it plunges into the river, lake, or ocean. Some older nestlings can glide for some distance, and the longer they are on the ground, the harder they will be to locate and return to the nest.

A Peregrine surveys the nest territory. —KATE DAVIS

7. Mammalian and Avian Predators

Scent trails left by humans may lead predators (raccoons, foxes, and ringtails, for example) straight to the nest if it is on or close to the ground. Francis Hammerstrom described the proper approach to a Northern Harrier nest as walking past it and retracing the way back, then coming in at a right angle. That last portion of the trail can be sprinkled with moth balls (naphthalene crystals) to mask human scent. Avian predators are not similarly tricked, and crows and ravens can eat the eggs and young of the smaller falcons.

After the visit, leave the territory entirely, walking out until you are sure the falcons are no longer affected by your presence. Very aggressive species such as Richardson's Merlins and Peregrines may "escort" human biologists some distance

A screaming Peregrine fledgling pursues the parent for an in-the-air food delivery of a pigeon.
—NICK DUNLOP

The parent Peregrine surrenders the prey. This post-fledging period is one of high mortality for the young birds.
—NICK DUNLOP

away, leaving the nest vulnerable. Fyfe and Olendorff warn, "Do not move off two hundred yards and stop to take notes."

8. Mishandling of Young Birds

Federal and state permits are required to enter or disturb any falcon nest, and extensive training is a prerequisite; the privilege should not be taken lightly. Obviously, unless a bird must be handled, don't do so. Make the observations from afar, collect the data, and leave. Nestlings of larger falcons (Gyrfalcon, Peregrine, Prairie) between fourteen and eighteen days of age may be easier to handle, but damage can still be done to chicks in all age groups. Legs, talons, wings, and feathers are easily damaged, and recently fed birds can suffer damage to their full crop. Both hands should be used in handling. When immobilizing chicks, grab them around the body and support their weight with your other hand between their legs. Prairie and Peregrine Falcon chicks can disappear into holes and inaccessible crevices, making them difficult to safely retrieve. Special care must be taken in freeing the falcon's talons from any substrate or a researcher's arm; the outer talon sheath is easily pulled off, and muscles and tendons can be damaged. Feathers that are actively growing are very fragile, and they emerge from the skin with a blood supply; damage can cause bleeding and irreparable injuries to the length of feather.

9. Miscellaneous Considerations

Other observation techniques can also lead to problems. Gyrfalcons and Peregrines sometimes deliberately strike helicopters and airplanes, posing a threat to themselves and the observers. Fyfe and Olendorff suggest protected airspace above the eyries of at least 1,500 feet (450 meters) with an approach from the front of the cliff; this allows the falcons time to step away from the eggs or chicks before they fly.

No more people should be at the nest site than is safe for the birds. One person can easily do the work if he or she knows the species, tasks, and his or her own abilities. Data can also be dictated to an assistant nearby. Preprinted cards or sheets speed up the process, but the best methodology is considerable experience. Just the pertinent data should be recorded at the nest itself. Other information (nesting sites, descriptions, and weather, for example) can be entered later away from the nest. When banding, birds generally should be at least one-half to two-thirds grown; the tarsus should be 95 percent developed, which is usually at two to three weeks of age.

Viewing conditions near the nest must also be taken into consideration for any observations of eggs or nestlings. When searching for new nest cliffs or attempting to ascertain occupancy at known sites, poor weather hinders observation and the safety of birds and observers. Precipitation, fog, wind, and heat waves can obscure viewing conditions and mask vocalizations, making viewing difficult or even impossible. After their morning activity, Peregrines sometimes sit tight on their cliff, or take advantage of afternoon thermals and winds to "lazily" hunt. By watching other raptors (vultures, buteos, eagles), observers can ascertain wind conditions aloft and roughly predict falcon and prey activity.

This paraglider was about to be struck by a Peregrine Falcon defending its nest. —WILL SOOTER

Observation points can be selected to allow some relief from direct sun and strong winds. Ideally, a view of a large portion of the cliff or other nest site and surrounding airspace allows for better observation of activity. Prime observation periods are usually at dawn; however, the aspect and angle of the sun may allow for better observation at a different time of day.

Nest observations for most falcons should encompass at least two four- to five-hour periods, twenty-five to thirty days apart. Determining fledging success often will require at least eight hours of additional observation (unless luck favors a quick ledge count). In other words, a great deal of time should be spent in the field. While concern is for the target species of falcon being observed, the observer must also consider factors to make his or her time safely and efficiently spent. High-quality optics are worth their weight in gold, and fine glass in binoculars and scopes is essential. Eye fatigue caused by poor optics or excessive strain of looking through a scope for longer than forty-five minutes leads to poorer-quality observations. To reduce fatigue and improve the quality of the observations, the researcher should be comfortable. Pagel suggests an item that might seem luxurious: a simple foam pad to sit on can make all the difference in comfort and hence support a more content researcher, who may make better-quality observations.

Any study (formal or informal) of raptor breeding biology should be approached in a thoughtful manner. Protocols must be established and adhered to, always with the safety and health of the birds (and observer) of utmost concern. All nest entries are restricted to experts only, permits in hand. Even what may seem to be casual observations or innocent disturbances can have disastrous effects. Self-discipline and thoughtful action should come naturally to falcon enthusiasts who wish to protect these birds—remarkable creatures that inspire such compassion, dedication, and respect.

Appendix 2

BUILDING AND PLACING AN AMERICAN KESTREL NEST BOX

American Kestrels are cavity nesters that return each spring to an area near where they were hatched. Where nest boxes are placed in the proper habitat, kestrel numbers have been shown to increase. A nesting pair produces 3 to 5 chicks. The young fledge at about a month and remain near the nest for a while. It is in late summer that we see these colorful and noisy birds hunting in family groups. Their prey is primarily rodents and insects, especially grasshoppers, so they are the farmer's best friend.

PLACING THE NEST BOX

+ Choose a site facing a large, open hunting ground—grassy fields, meadows, or farmland—with nearby perches. Keep the box in plain view with few limbs in front.

+ Hang box 10-30 feet high on a pole, snag, or tree, preferably facing south to east. Do not attach boxes to power poles; it is dangerous and against the law.

+ Males are territorial, so don't place boxes closer than 1/4 mile apart.

+ It is a good idea to wrap the pole or tree with 2 feet of metal or aluminum flashing about 5 feet above the ground to prevent raccoons from raiding the nest.

+ Place several inches of wood shavings inside the box; shavings should be replaced each year.

+ If the box is not used for three years, move it to another location.

+ Starlings may occupy the nest box; they are an invasive species and harm native birds, so the eggs may be removed.

American Kestrel Nest Box

This plan modified from kestrel nest box plan featured in *Woodworking for Wildlife: Homes for Birds and Mammals* (Published by Minnesota DNR; Carrol Henderson, author)

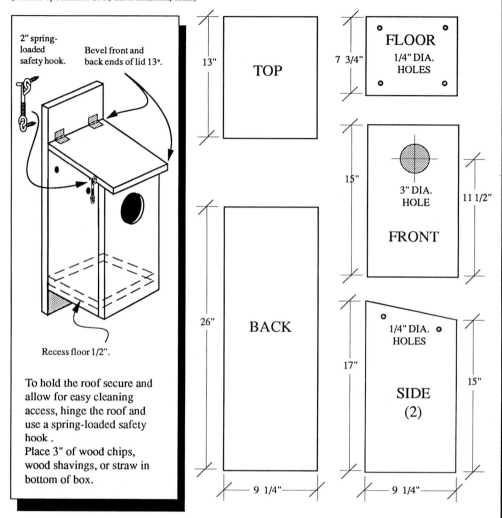

2" spring-loaded safety hook.

Bevel front and back ends of lid 13°.

TOP — 13"

FLOOR — 7 3/4", 1/4" DIA. HOLES

FRONT — 15", 3" DIA. HOLE, 11 1/2"

BACK — 26", 9 1/4"

SIDE (2) — 17", 15", 1/4" DIA. HOLES, 9 1/4"

Recess floor 1/2".

To hold the roof secure and allow for easy cleaning access, hinge the roof and use a spring-loaded safety hook.
Place 3" of wood chips, wood shavings, or straw in bottom of box.

LUMBER: One 1" x 10" x 8' 0", (#2 white pine recommend). Painting the box will increase its useful life.
HARDWARE: Twenty-two 1 1/2" wood screws (#6), two 2" hinges and one 2" spring-loaded safety hook.

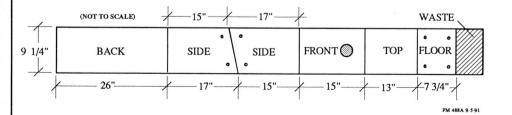

(NOT TO SCALE)

9 1/4"

BACK — 26" | SIDE — 17" | SIDE — 15" | FRONT — 15" | TOP — 13" | FLOOR — 7 3/4" | WASTE

15" — 17"

PM 488A 9-5-91

Glossary

allopreen. To groom the feathers of another bird, usually in courtship.

altricial. Said of newly hatched chicks that are born with eyes closed, featherless, and entirely reliant on one or both parents for food and warmth.

alula (pl. alulae). The group of feathers at the "thumb" of the wing that helps maintain a smooth flow of air across the upper wing surface; bastard wing.

aspect ratio. In simple terms, the proportion of wing length to surface area; falcon wings have a high aspect ratio: long and narrow.

asynchronous hatch. When eggs hatch days apart, so there are chicks of different ages and stages of development in the nest simultaneously.

auricular. Having to do with the area around a bird's ear; also describes the stiff feathers that cover the ear openings.

binocular vision. Informally, having two forward-facing eyes with an overlapping field of vision, which the brain fuses into a single image, allowing for greater depth perception; common in predators.

brood (n). A group of nestlings from the same breeding cycle; clutch.

brood (v). To shelter nestlings from the elements or predators, as with wings.

cache. To store uneaten portions of food in a hidden place for later consumption.

camber. The upward curve in a structure. Falcons have low wing camber, with wings held fairly flat.

casting. The indigestible parts of a meal, such as fur and bones, that are coughed up in the form of a compact ball; pellet.

cere. The bare patch of skin around the beak and nostrils.

clutch. The total number of eggs laid by a female in a single breeding cycle.

convergent evolution. The process by which unrelated groups of animals evolve similar physical or behavioral traits in order to perform similar functions in similar environments, such as hunting in open terrain.

cosmopolitan. Describes a species or other group that lives all around the world.

coverts. The small feathers that cover the bases of the flight feathers

crop. A pouch in the throat of most birds that temporarily stores food before it moves into the first stomach.

dispersal. Usually pertains to movement of young birds away from the nest area.

diurnal. Active during daylight hours.

DDT (dichloro-diphenyl-trichloroethane). A synthetic pesticide used to kill mosquitoes and other insects; banned since the 1970s in the United States due to its harmful effects on raptors and other birds.

emarginated. Said of a wing feather that has slotting or narrowing on the outer edge; on the inner edge the feather is said to be "notched."

estivate. To retreat underground to escape summer heat, like hibernating in summer; some ground squirrels, for example, do this.

extirpation. This occurs when a species or population becomes extinct in a portion of its historical range, but continues to live and breed elsewhere.

eyas. A young raptor chick that is still in the nest.

eyrie. The cliff or ledge nest of raptors such as falcons or Golden Eagles; aerie.

Falco. The genus of true falcons

Falconidae. The family of falcons, forest-falcons, and caracaras.

Falconiformes. The order of birds that includes falcons, hawks, eagles, Ospreys, Old World vultures, and Secretary Birds.

feak. A falconry term for a bird cleaning its beak by rubbing it on a limb, rock, or whatever they are standing on, especially after feeding.

fledging. The time when a young bird leaves the nest, often still fed by parents; the term can also refer to growing the first set of flight feathers and learning to fly.

flicker fusion frequency. The number of still images per second that the brain perceives as continuous motion rather than as separate visual images.

floater. An unmated adult bird that may substitute if one bird in a pair is killed during breeding season.

follicle. The small, round structure on a bird's skin that grows a feather.

fovea. A depression on the interior surface of the eye where the image is focused and magnified.

hack. To release a young bird from an enclosure where it continually fed until it gains independence; used in bird reintroduction programs.

hallux. The hind toe of most birds.

hyperphagia. Excessive eating, as some raptors do to store energy prior to migration.

irruption. A temporary population explosion; in birds, it is movement of out of a normal range for the season, often associated with cycles of prey availability.

juvenal. Describes the first full set of feathers of a juvenile bird.

juvenile. The young of an animal before reaching breeding age.

keratin. Proteins that are components of skin, beaks, scales, feathers, and talons.

kettle. A group of raptors soaring and circling together in a thermal.

kleptoparasitism. Stealing food from another animal; also called pirating.

malar stripe. A darkened stripe or a patch in the cheek area of a bird.

mantle (n). The upper back and scapular region of a bird.

mantle (v). To hide an object, such as food or a falconry lure, with outstretched wings, spread tail, and a hunkering posture.

manus. The "hand" region of a wing; a falcon's ten primary feathers are attached to the bones of the manus.

maxilla. The upper jaw.

migration. The movement of a population from one area to another; usually refers to seasonal migration north and south, but can be altitudinal.

mobbing. Defensive behavior of prey birds, often in flocks, flying directly at a predator and noisily indicating that danger is present.

molt. Seasonal feather loss and replacement; raptors molt flight and contour feathers over the summer.

morphology. The study of structure and anatomy in animals.

motion parallax. The phenomenon in which an object seems to move against a stationary background as the viewer's position changes. By bobbing its head a falcon can see a potential prey animal from many different angles and judge the distance.

nares. The nostrils of a bird.

nictitating membrane. The third eyelid, or inner eyelid, of all birds; it keeps the eye moist and protects the surface.

nidicolous. Describes a young bird that remains in the nest for some time, totally dependent on parent birds for brooding and feeding.

nominant. The subspecies for which the first descriptions of a species were made.

ocelli. The plumage that creates the "false eyes" present on the posterior region of the head of the American Kestrel and Northern Pygmy-owl.

order. The scientific group below class; in birds the class Aves contains about two dozen orders, including the two raptor orders, Falconiformes and Strigiformes (owls).

passerine. A bird of the order Passeriformes, the perching birds, which includes songbirds.

pellet. The compact ball of indigestible prey parts that is regurgitated sometime after a meal; for owls it is bones covered by fur or feathers; for hawks and falcons there are fewer bones, and the pellet is commonly called a casting.

philopatry. Nest site fidelity, or the tendency of a bird to return to the vicinity where it was raised as a youngster.

photoperiod. The length of daylight hours, which changes seasonally

preen. To straighten, clean, and waterproof the feathers by drawing them through the beak and adding oil from the uropygial, or oil, gland at the base of the tail.

primaries. The ten flight feathers attached to the manus, or "hand," of the wing.

pygostyle. The fused bones of a bird's tail, to which the tail feathers and muscles attach.

range. The geographic region that an animal is found in at a certain time of year, as in winter range, breeding range, year-round range.

raptor. Bird of prey, from the Latin word *raptare*, for "seize and carry away"; includes both the orders of hawks and owls.

recruitment. Young produced to replace older birds in a population as they die, expressed as recruitment rate or standard.

rectrices. The flight feathers of the tail, numbering twelve on a falcon.

remiges. The flight feathers of the wing; primaries and secondaries.

reticulate foot. Found in falcons and plovers; a foot on which the scales are small, irregular, and netlike, or reticulated.

scrape. The slight depression in the gravel, sand, or soil of the ledge that makes up a falcon nest, made by the parents scraping loose debris away with their feet.

secondaries. The flight feathers attached to the forearm region of the wing.

sexual dimorphism. A physical difference between the sexes, such as size or color; most raptors exhibit reverse sexual size dimorphism, in which the female is larger than the male.

stoop. The fast downward, sometimes completely vertical, flight of a hunting falcon.

subspecies. A variation, usually geographic, of a species, differing in appearance or behavior, but able to breed with other subspecies where they occur together.

synchronous hatch. When the young in a nest all hatch more or less at the same time; occurs in species that do not begin incubation until all of the eggs in a clutch have been laid.

taiga. The habitat type encompassing northern latitudes just south of the Arctic tundra, with primarily coniferous forest; from the Russian word for this forest.

talon. The curved "claw" on the toe of a bird of prey.

thermal. The rising current of air created when ground air is heated, creating soaring conditions for many birds.

thermoregulate. The ability to maintain one's own body temperature.

tiercel. A falconry term for a male falcon.

tomial notch. A notch on the beak of falcons to help break the neck of a prey animal.

uropygial gland. The oil gland at the base of the tail, used in preening and water-proofing the feathers.

wing loading. The proportion of a bird's weight, or body mass, to the surface area of the wings. Falcons have high wing loading, meaning they are relatively heavy in relation to their long, narrow wings, equipping them for high-speed flight.

References

Agassiz Fuertes, L. 1920. "Falconry, the Sport of Kings," *National Geographic* 38: 429-60.

_____. 1905. A note on the Prairie Falcon. *Condor* 7:35-36.

Baker, J. A. 1986. *Peregrine*. Moscow, ID: Idaho Research Foundation.

Anderson, S. H., and J. R. Squires. 1997. *The Prairie Falcon*. Austin: University of Texas Press.

Beebe, F. L., and H. M. Webster. 2000. *North American falconry and hunting hawks*. Topeka, Kans.: Josten's Printing and Publishing Division.

Bent, A. C. 1937. *Life histories of North American birds of prey: Falcons, hawks, caracaras, owls*. New York: Dover Publications.

Bevanger, K. 1994. Bird interactions with utility structures: Collisions and electrocution, causes and mitigating measures. *Ibis* 136:412-25.

_____. 1998. Biological and conservation aspects of bird mortality caused by electricity power lines: A review. *Biological Conservation* 86:67-76.

Bildstein, K. L. 2006. *Migrating raptors of the world: Their ecology and conservation*. Ithaca, N.Y.: Comstock Publishing Associates, Cornell University Press.

Bildstein, K. L., and D. Klem Jr., eds. 2001. *Hawkwatching in the Americas*. North Wales, Penn.: Hawk Migration Association of North America.

Bird, D., and R. Bowman, eds. 1987. *The ancestral kestrel*. Ste. Anne de Bellevue, Quebec: Raptor Research Foundation and Macdonald Raptor Research Centre of McGill University.

Bird, D., D. Varland, and J. Negro, eds. 1996. *Raptors in human landscapes: Adaptations to built and cultivated environments*. San Diego, Calif.: Academic Press.

Bond, R. M. 1946. The Peregrine population of western North America. *Condor* 48: 101-16

Boyce, D. A., and C. W. White. 1987. "Evolutionary aspects of kestrel systematics: A scenario in the ancestral kestrel." In *The Ancestral Kestrel*, ed. D. Bird and R. Bowman. Ste. Anne de Bellevue, Quebec: Raptor Research Foundation and Macdonald Raptor Research Centre of McGill University.

Brach, V. 1977. The functional significance of the avian pectin: A review. *Condor* 79:321-27.

215

Brown, L. 1976. *Birds of prey: Their biology and ecology*. Middlesex, England: Hamlyn.

Brown, L., and D. Amadon. 1989. *Eagles, hawks and falcons of the world*. Secaucus, N.J.: Wellfleet Press.

Brown, J. L., M. W. Collopy, et al. 2006. Wild-reared Aplomado Falcons survive and recruit at higher rates than hacked falcons in a common environment. *Biological Conservation* 131:453-58.

Bub, H. 1991. *Bird trapping and banding: A handbook for trapping methods all over the world*. Ithaca, N.Y.: Cornell University Press.

Cade, T. J. *The falcons of the world*. 1982. Ithaca, N.Y.: Comstock Publishing Associates, Cornell University Press.

Cade, T. J., and W. Burnham, eds. 2003. *Return of the Peregrine: A North American saga of tenacity and teamwork*. Boise, Idaho: The Peregrine Fund.

Cade, T. J., J. H. Enderson, C. G. Thelander, and C. M. White, eds. 1988. *Peregrine Falcon populations: Their management and recovery*. Boise, Idaho: The Peregrine Fund.

Campbell, B., and E. Lack. 1985. *A dictionary of birds*. Berkhamsted, England: T. & A. D. Poyser.

Clark, W. S., and B. K. Wheeler. 1987. *Peterson field guide: Hawks*. Boston: Houghton Mifflin.

Clay, W. M. 1953. Protective coloration in the American Sparrow Hawk. *Wilson Bulletin* 65: 129-34.

Clum, N. J., and T. J. Cade. 1994. *Gyrfalcon* (Falco rusticolus). In *The birds of North America*, no. 114, ed. A. Poole and F. Gill. Philadephia, Penn.: The Academy of Natural Sciences.

Cochran, W. W., and R. D. Applegate. 1986. Speed of flapping flight of Merlins and Peregrine Falcons. *Condor* 88:397-98.

Cox, R. T. 1996. *Birder's dictionary*. Helena, Mont.: Falcon Press.

Craighead, J. J., and F. C. 1937. "Adventures with birds of prey." *National Geographic* 72: 109-34.

————. 1939. *Hawks in the hand: Adventures in photography and falconry*. New York: Houghton Mifflin.

————. 1969. *Hawks, owls, and wildlife*. New York: Dover Publications. Reprint of 1956 edition.

————. 1942. "Life with an Indian Prince." *National Geographic*. 81.

Crick, H. Q. P. 2004. The impact of climate change on birds. *Ibis* 146:48-56.

de Chamerlat, C. A. 1987. *Falconry and art*. London: Sotheby's Publications.

Dekker, D. 1999. *Bolt from the blue: Wild Peregrines on the hunt*. Blaine, Wash.: Hancock House Publishers.

del Hoyo, J., A. Elliott, and J. Sargatal, eds. 1994. *Handbook of the birds of the world. Volume 2: New World vultures to guineafowl.* Barcelona: Lynx Edicions.

Department of the Interior, U. S. Fish and Wildlife Service. 1976. Falconry regulations set. News Release Jan. 16.

Drewitt, A. L., and R. H. W. Langston. 2006. Assessing the impacts of wind farms on birds. *Ibis* 148:29-42.

Dunne, P., D. Keller, R. Kochenberger, and D. Sibley. 1984. *Hawk watch: A guide for beginners.* Cape May, N.J.: Cape May Bird Observatory/New Jersey Audubon Society.

Dunne, P., D. Sibley, and C. Sutton. 1988. *Hawks in flight.* Boston: Houghton Mifflin.

Enderson, J. H. 2005. *Peregrine Falcon: Stories of the blue meanie.* Austin: University of Texas Press.

Ferguson-Lees, J., and D. A. Christie. 2001. *Raptors of the world.* Boston: Houghton Mifflin Company.

Fox, N. 1995. *Understanding the bird of prey.* Blaine, Wash.: Hancock House Publishers.

Franklin, K. 1999. Vertical flight. *North American Falconers' Association Journal* 38:68-72.

Fyfe, R. W., and R. R. Olendorff. 1976. Minimizing the dangers of nesting studies to raptors and other sensitive species. Occasional Paper no. 23, Canadian Wildlife Service.

Gill, F. B. 1995. *Ornithology.* New York: W. H. Freeman and Company.

Goede, A. A., and M. De Bruin. 2004. The use of bird feathers for indicating heavy metal pollution. *Environmental Monitoring and Assessment* 7:249-256..

Grossman, M. L., and J. Hamlet. 1964. *Birds of prey of the world.* New York: C.N. Potter.

Hackett, S. J., Kimball, R. T., et al. 2008. "A phylogenomic study of birds reveals their evolutionary history." Science 320: 1763-1768.

Harrison, H. H. 1979. *Peterson field guides: Western birds' nests.* Boston: Houghton Mifflin.

Hickey, J. J. 1942. Eastern population of the Duck Hawk. *Auk* 59: 176-204.

Hobson, K. A. 1999. Tracing origins and migration of wildlife using stable isotopes: A review. *Oecologia* 120:314-26.

Jameson, E. W., and H. J. Peeters. 1971. *An introduction to hawking.* Davis, Calif.: The Printer.

Johnsgard, P. A. 1990. *Hawks, eagles and falcons of North America: Biology and natural history.* Washington, D.C.: Smithsonian Institution Press.

Keddy-Hector, D. P. 2000. *Aplomado Falcon* (Falco femoralis). In *The birds of North America,* no. 549, ed. A. Poole and F. Gill. Philadephia, Penn.: The Birds of North America, Inc.

Kerlinger, P. 1989. *Flight strategies of migrating hawks.* Chicago: University of Chicago Press.

Lehman, R. N. 2001. Raptor electrocution on power lines: Current issues and outlook. *Wildlife Society Bulletin* 29:804-13.

Lehman, R., B. Walton, and L. Spiegel. 2006. Raptor electrocution on power lines: Problem assessment, mitigation, and monitoring. PIER Energy-Related Environmental Research, Sacramento, Calif.

Liguori, J. 2005. *Hawks from every angle: How to identify raptors in flight.* Princeton, N.J.: Princeton University Press.

Louv, R. 2008. *Last Child in the Woods.* Chapel Hill, NC: Algonquin Books.

Macdonald, H. 2001. *Falcon.* London: Reaktion Books.

Meredith, R. L. 1999. *American Falconry in the Twentieth Century.* Boise, ID: Archives of American Falconry.

Mills, H. B. 1937. *Some Montana birds: Their relationship to insects and rodents.* Bozeman, Mont.: Montana State College Agricultural Experiment Station.

Millsap, B. A., and G. T. Allen. 2006. Effects of falconry harvest on wild raptor populations in the United States: Theoretical considerations and management recommendations. *Wildlife Society Bulletin* 35:1392-1400.

National Geographic Society. 1999. *Field guide to the birds of North America.* Third Edition. Washington, D.C.: National Geographic.

Newton, I. 1979. *Population ecology of raptors.* Berkhamsted, England: T. & A. D. Poyser.

_____. 2008. *The migration ecology of birds.* Burlington, Mass.: Academic Press.

Newton, I., and P. Olsen. 1990. *Birds of prey.* New York: Facts on File, Inc.

Oggins, R. S. 2004. *The kings and their hawks: Falconry in medieval England.* New Haven: Yale University Press.

Orloff, S., and A. Flannery. 1992. Wind turbine effects on avian activity, habitat use, and mortality in Altamont Pass and Solano County. Biosystems Analysis, Inc., Sacramento, Calif.

Pagel, J. E. 1991. Protocol for observing known and potential Peregrine Falcon eyries in the Pacific Northwest. In *Proceedings: Symposium on Peregrine Falcons* in the Pacific Northwest, ed. J. Pagel. Medford, Ore: Rogue River National Forest.

Parry-Jones, J. 1988. *Jemima Parry-Jones' falconry: Care, captive breeding and conservation.* Devon, England: David and Charles.

Paulson, D. E. 1985. The importance of open habitat to the occurrence of kleptoparasitism. *Auk* 102: 637-39.

Pearson, G. T. 1936. *Birds of America.* Garden City, N.Y.: Garden City Publishing, Inc.

Peeters, H. J. 2005. *Raptors of California.* Berkeley: University of California Press.

Peterson, R. T. 1947. *A field guide to the birds: Eastern land and water birds*. Boston: Houghton Mifflin.

Potapov, E., and R. Sale. 2005. *The Gyrfalcon*. New Haven, Conn.: Yale University Press.

Proctor, N. S., and P. J. Lynch. 1993. *Manual of ornithology: Avian structure and function*. New Haven, Conn.: Yale University Press.

Ratcliffe, D. 1980. *The Peregrine Falcon*. Berkhamsted, England: T. & A. D. Poyser.

Sanz, J. J. 2002. Climate change and birds: Have their ecological consequences already been detected in the Mediterranean region? *Ardeola* 49:109-20.

Sherrod, S. K. 1983. *Behavior of fledgling Peregrines*. Fort Collins, Colo.: Pioneer Impressions.

Sibley, D. A. 2000. *The Sibley guide to bird life and behavior*. New York: Alfred A. Knopf.

————. 2000. *The Sibley guide to birds*. New York: Alfred A. Knopf.

Smallwood, J. A., and D. M. Bird. 2002. *American Kestrel* (Falco sparverius). In *The birds of North America*, no. 602, ed. A. Poole and F. Gill. Philadephia, Penn.: The Birds of North America, Inc.

Smallwood, K. S., and C. G. Thelander. 2005. Bird mortality at Altamont Pass Wind Resource Area, March 1998-Sept. 2001, National Renewable Energy Laboratory, U.S. Department of Energy.

Sodhi, N. S., L. W. Oliphant, P. C. James, and I. G. Warkentin. 1993. *Merlin* (Falco columbarius). In *The birds of North America*, no. 602, ed. A. Poole and F. Gill. Philadephia, Penn.: The Academy of Natural Sciences.

Steenhof, K. 1998. *Prairie Falcon* (Falco mexicanus). In *The birds of North America*, no. 346, ed. A. Poole and F. Gill. Philadephia, Penn.: The Birds of North America, Inc.

Steenhof, K., M. R. Fuller, M. N. Kochert, and K. K. Bates. 2005. Long-range movements and breeding dispersal of Prairie Falcons from southwest Idaho. *Condor* 107:481-96.

Steenhof, K., M. R. Fuller, M.N. Kochert, L. B. Carpenter, and R. N. Lehman. 1999. Long-term Prairie Falcon population changes in relation to prey abundance, weather, land uses, and habitat conditions. *Condor* 101:28-41.

Sturkie, P. D., ed. 1976. *Avian physiology*. New York: Springer-Verlag.

Sutton, C., and P. T. Sutton. 1996. *How to spot hawks and eagles*. Boston: Houghton Mifflin.

Svensson, L., and P. J. Grant. 1999. *Collins bird guide*. London: Harper Collins.

Tucker, V. A. 1998. Gliding flight: Speed and acceleration of ideal falcons during diving and pull out. *Journal of Experimental Biology* 201:403-14.

————. 2000. The deep fovea, sideways vision and spiral flight paths in raptors. *Journal of Experimental Biology* 203:3745-54.

_____. 2000. Gliding flight: Drag and torque of a hawk and falcon with straight and turned heads, and a lower value for parasite drag coefficient. *Journal of Experimental Biology* 203:3733-44.

Tucker, V. A., T. J. Cade, and A. E. Tucker. 1998. Diving speeds and angles of a Gyrfalcon (*Falco rusticolus*). *Journal of Experimental Biology* 201:2061-70.

U.S. Department of the Interior, U.S. Geologic Survey. 1999-2001. *Manual of wildlife diseases: General field procedures and diseases of birds.* Washington, D.C.: Biological Resources Division, Information and Technology Report.

Varland, D. E., E. R. Klass, and T. M. Loughin. 1991. Development of foraging behavior in the American Kestrel. *Journal of Raptor Research* 25:9-17.

Varland, D. E., and T. M. Loughin. 1993. Reproductive success of American Kestrels nesting along an interstate highway in central Iowa. *Wilson Bulletin* 105:465-74.

Visser, M. E., and C. Both. 2005. Shifts in phenology due to global climate change: The need for a yardstick. *Proceedings of the Royal Society B* 272:2561-69.

Weidensaul, S. 1996. *Raptors: Birds of prey.* New York: Lyons & Burford.

Welty, J. C. 1962. *The life of birds.* Philadelphia: W. B. Saunders Company.

Wheeler, B. K. 2007. *Raptors of Eastern North America.* Princeton, NJ: Princeton University Press.

_____. 2007. *Raptors of Western North America.* Princeton, NJ: Princeton University Press.

Wheeler, B. K., and W. S. Clark. 1995. *A photographic guide to North American raptors.* San Diego, Calif.: Academic Press.

White, C. 2006. *Peregrine quest: From a naturalist's field notebooks.* Ranchester, Wyo.: Western Sporting.

White, C. M., N. J. Clum, T. J. Cade, and G. Hunt. 2002. *Peregrine Falcon* (Falco peregrinus). In *The birds of North America*, no. 660, eds. A. Poole and F. Gill. Philadephia, Penn.: The Birds of North America, Inc.

Wilkinson, J. 2006. Bird radar to test airplane strikes. *Air Force Print News.* Nov. 1, 2006.

Zalles, J. I., and K. L. Bildstein, eds. 2000. *Raptor watch: A global directory of raptor migration sites.* Cambridge: Birdlife International; Kempton, Penn.: Hawk Mountain Sanctuary.

Index

Boldface page numbers refer to photographs or illustrations.